A Guide to
Biltmore Estate

THE BILTMORE COMPANY

ASHEVILLE, NORTH CAROLINA

© 2001 The Biltmore Company

Published by The Biltmore Company
One North Pack Square, Asheville, North Carolina 28801
800-543-2961 or 828-255-1700

Produced by
Rosemary G. Rennicke, Buckingham, Pennsylvania, and
Diane Maddex, Archetype Press, Inc., Washington, D.C.
Original Text written by Rachel D. Carley and Rosemary G. Rennicke
Designed by Marc Alain Meadows and Robert L. Wiser, Archetype Press, Inc.
Project coordination at Biltmore Estate by Julia Weede, Jane Cox Murray, Judy Ross, Elizabeth Pendleton, Christy Cowan.
Color photographs by Bill Alexander, Tim Barnwell, Richard Brown and Assoc., Cheryl Dalton,
Terry Davis, Carroll Morgan, Mike Smith, Sandra Stambaugh, James Valentine, and John Warner.
Black-and-white photographs from Biltmore Estate archives.

Library of Congress Cataloging-in-Publication Data
Carley, Rachel.
A guide to Biltmore Estate / [written by Rachel Carley and Rosemary G. Rennicke].
    p.   cm.
ISBN 1-885378-00-9 (hardbound). — ISBN 1-885378-01-7 (paperbound)
1. Biltmore Estate (Asheville, N.C.) — Guidebooks.   2. Asheville (N.C.) — Buildings, structures, etc. —
Guidebooks.   I. Title.
F264.A8C36   1994   94-11621
975.6′88—dc20   CIP

Front cover photo by James Valentine. Copyright page: George Vanderbilt's bookplate.
Back cover (clockwise from top left): Biltmore's Shrub Garden, Italian Garden, Biltmore House
from the Lagoon (by James Valentine), and Bass Pond bridge.

Printed in China

I NEVER KNEW MY GREAT-GRANDFATHER, GEORGE VANDERBILT, but I cherish the memories of him that have been passed down through the family. I know, for example, his vision for Biltmore was one of a self-sufficient estate, where a home equipped with cutting-edge technology of the day would stand at the center of a carefully designed working farm and a beautiful park and woods. I know, too, that he loved to travel. He filled Biltmore House with the treasures he brought back from England, Italy, France, and Asia. And most of all, I know he took special pride in sharing his home with others. From the first day Biltmore was opened, on Christmas Eve in 1895, it was often host to family and friends—everyone from famous artists to neighborhood children.

Guests remain a central part of the estate today. Each one of you keeps alive the pleasure my great-grandfather took in entertaining and maintains his ideal of a private working estate that sustains itself and benefits the community. As we embark upon new projects, such as the Inn on Biltmore Estate, we appreciate your support that allows Biltmore to remain self-sufficient and to lead the way in historic preservation through private enterprise.

I know my great-grandfather would be pleased that so many people continue to visit his home—and perpetuate his dream. I hope, as you tour the estate, and extend your experience by a stay at the inn, that you enjoy yourself as thoroughly as the honored guests who have preceded you. And that you take home memories as precious as my own.

Welcome to Biltmore Estate.

Bill Cecil, Jr.

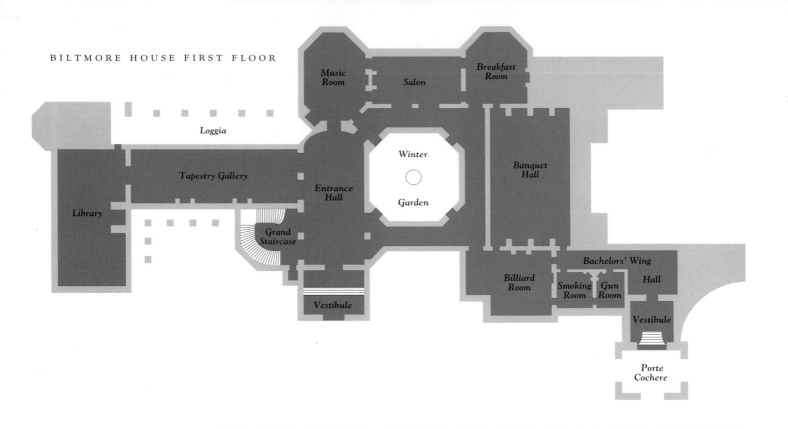

BILTMORE HOUSE FIRST FLOOR

Music Room

Salon

Breakfast Room

Loggia

Winter Garden

Banquet Hall

Tapestry Gallery

Entrance Hall

Library

Grand Staircase

Bachelors' Wing

Billiard Room

Smoking Room

Gun Room

Hall

Vestibule

Vestibule

Porte Cochere

Contents

Mr. Vanderbilt's Bedroom

Oak Sitting Room

Mrs. Vanderbilt's Bedroom

Bath

Sheraton Room

Chippendale Room

Old English Room

Second Floor Living Hall

Grand Staircase

Louis XVI Room

BILTMORE HOUSE SECOND FLOOR

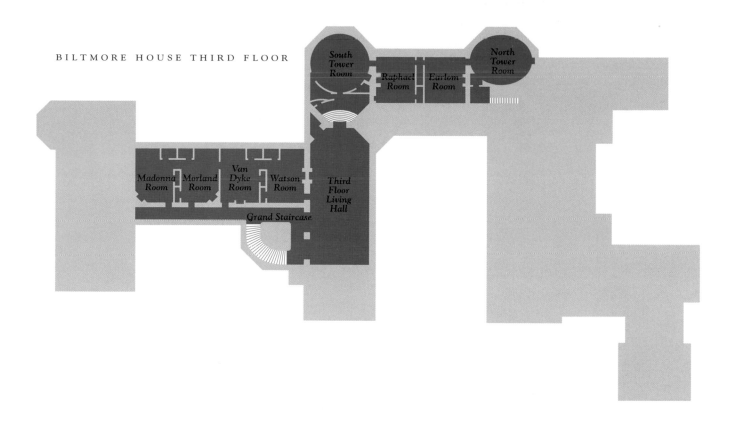

BILTMORE HOUSE THIRD FLOOR

South Tower Room
Raphael Room
Earlom Room
North Tower Room
Madonna Room
Morland Room
Van Dyke Room
Watson Room
Third Floor Living Hall
Grand Staircase

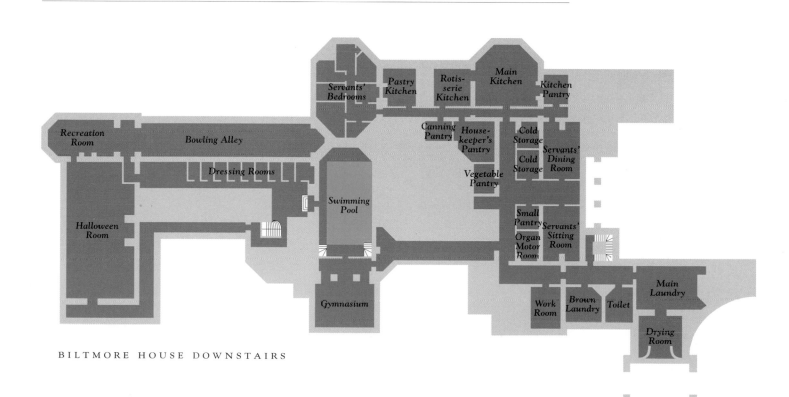

Servants' Bedrooms
Pastry Kitchen
Rotisserie Kitchen
Main Kitchen
Kitchen Pantry
Recreation Room
Bowling Alley
Canning Pantry
Housekeeper's Pantry
Cold Storage
Servants' Dining Room
Dressing Rooms
Cold Storage
Vegetable Pantry
Swimming Pool
Small Pantry
Servants' Sitting Room
Halloween Room
Organ Motor Room
Gymnasium
Work Room
Brown Laundry
Toilet
Main Laundry
Drying Room

BILTMORE HOUSE DOWNSTAIRS

The Story of Biltmore

BILTMORE ESTATE IS A TESTAMENT to the uncompromising ideals of an exceptional man—George Washington Vanderbilt. What began as his vision of a country retreat became the largest private residence in America. It stands to this day as a celebrated historic landmark. To visit Biltmore is to cross the threshold into a world of hospitality, beauty, and luxury that has remained unchanged for more than a century and is being preserved for many generations yet to come.

*W*HEN GEORGE WASHINGTON VANDERBILT III WELCOMED family and friends to Biltmore Estate on Christmas Eve in 1895, his holiday celebration marked the formal opening of the most ambitious home ever conceived in America. For six years, an army of artisans had labored to create a country estate that would rival the great manors of Europe and embody the finest in architecture, landscape planning, and interior design. The results were astounding.

Boasting four acres of floor space, the 250-room mansion featured 34 family and guest bedrooms, 43 bathrooms, 65 fireplaces, three kitchens, and an indoor swimming pool. It was appointed with a priceless collection of furnishings and artworks and equipped with every conceivable amenity, from elevators to refrigerators. The surrounding grounds were equally impressive, encompassing a 100,000-acre forest, several large farms, a 250-acre wooded park, five pleasure gardens, and 30 miles of macadamized roadways.

The youngest in a family renowned for building palatial homes, 33-year-old George Vanderbilt had outdone them all.

A FAMILY LEGACY The Vanderbilts were not only one of the best-known families in America, but they were also among the oldest: Jan Aertsen van der Bilt had emigrated to this country from Holland around 1650. Although his descendants prospered as farmers on Staten Island, New York, they lived modestly; it was only during the lifetime of Cornelius Vanderbilt (1794–1877) that the family name became synonymous with extraordinary wealth.

Legend holds that Cornelius changed the family fortune at age 16 with a $100 loan from his mother. Strong willed and self-educated, the budding entrepreneur

OPPOSITE: George Vanderbilt, seen in a turn-of-the-century photograph on display in the Tapestry Gallery, was only 33 years old when he opened Biltmore. ABOVE: The Estate as it appeared in the late 1890s. It remains the largest private residence in America.

ABOVE: *A patron of the arts and a collector of fine paintings, William Henry Vanderbilt commissioned* Going to the Opera—Family Portrait *from the American artist Seymour Guy in 1873. William Henry is seated at the left and is surrounded by his wife, their eight children, and other family members. George Vanderbilt is the young boy seated in front of his father.*

launched a ferry service across New York Bay, which he eventually parlayed into a fleet of more than 100 steamboats that traveled as far as Central America and Europe. Some 50 years later, the "Commodore," as he came to be called, earned his second fortune investing in railroads, the fabled New York Central among them. He began the Vanderbilt tradition of philanthropy, contributing $1 million in 1873 to Central University, a Methodist school in Nashville; it was renamed Vanderbilt University.

The Commodore was the patriarch of a sizable family—including his wife of 53 years, Sophia, 13 children, 37 grandchildren, and 27 great-grandchildren. Upon his death the Commodore left most of his $100 million estate—a sum that made him the wealthiest industrialist of his time—to his eldest son, William Henry (1821–85). Although his father had once considered him unsuited to business, William Henry took over the family empire and eventually doubled his assets. He, too, was generous toward worthy causes, funding the Metropolitan Opera in 1883 and endowing the College of Physicians and Surgeons, now the Medical School of Columbia University.

The shrewd financier proved to be an equally astute collector, assembling more

The Vanderbilt Family

The Vanderbilts are a large family descended in America from Jan Aertsen van der Bilt, who emigrated from Holland around 1650. The first family member to gain prominence was Cornelius, known as the "Commodore," who married Sophia Johnson in 1813 (both, top row, at left). Their eldest son was William Henry, who in 1841 married Maria Louisa Kissam (both, top row, at right). Their youngest child was George Washington, who wed Edith Stuyvesant Dresser in 1898 (both, at left). They had one child, Cornelia Stuyvesant (below left), who married John Cecil in 1924. The younger of their two sons is William A.V. Cecil, shown with his wife, children, and grandchildren (below right).

ABOVE: *George Vanderbilt around 1874.* BELOW LEFT: *George's travel diary from 1880, when he sailed to Europe aboard the steamship* Brittanic *for a five-month tour of Italy, England, France, Switzerland, and Germany.* BELOW RIGHT: *Mr. Vanderbilt (seated, rear) cruised along the canals of Venice in the 1890s; the Doge's Palace and the Piazza San Marco are in the background.*

than 200 paintings. These were displayed in the 58-room mansion he built in 1881 at 640 Fifth Avenue—the largest and most splendid house in Manhattan at that time. Outfitted with all the latest conveniences, such as telephones and refrigeration, the house was exquisitely decorated with European furniture, tapestries, stained-glass windows, and countless art objects; it also had a glass-roofed stable courtyard so his beloved trotting horses could exercise without being exposed to the weather.

Only one of the eight children of William Henry and his wife, Maria Louisa (1821–96), was still living at home when the house was completed: the youngest, George, born in 1862. Quiet and intellectual, he had been greatly influenced by his father's cultural interests, starting his own collection of art and books at an early age; he even oversaw the design of his private quarters, including a library, in the new mansion. Significantly, George Vanderbilt would inherit the house and its contents after his mother's death.

Unlike the his older brothers, however, Mr. Vanderbilt was little attracted to the family business. He preferred the world of learning and travel, taking his first trip to Europe at age 10 and journeying to Europe, Asia, or Africa about once a year throughout his adult life. It was while traveling in the mountains of North Carolina that Mr. Vanderbilt first glimpsed his destiny.

A VISION UNFOLDS Asheville was a popular health resort in the late 19th century, when train service brought tourists into the southern Appalachians to enjoy the mineral springs, fresh air, and pleasant climate. When George Vanderbilt visited in 1888 with his mother, he was captivated by the rugged beauty of the rural region and found it the perfect setting for a new home.

Here he could fulfill his vision for an estate—one that would serve not only as a showcase for his cherished collections and a retreat for entertaining but also as a profitable, self-supporting business. He based his concept on the vast landed baronies he had seen in Europe, where country estates had endured for centuries, preserving both family and national heritage. He was also influenced by the Vanderbilt tradition of extravagant homes and by the 3,500-acre Vermont estate, Shelburne Farms, that his sister Lila and her husband, William Seward Webb, had created in 1886.

ABOVE: *Biltmore Estate was the result of a collaboration among three talented men: Richard Morris Hunt (standing, second from left), George Washington Vanderbilt (standing, right), and Frederick Law Olmsted (sitting, center).*

Taking the first step toward his goal, Mr. Vanderbilt began purchasing parcels of land—which was both affordable and readily available in this area—eventually amassing 125,000 acres, including the 100,000-acre tract which became Pisgah Forest. He called his estate "Biltmore"—from Bildt, the Dutch town where his ancestors originated, and "more," an old English word for open, rolling land. He then engaged two of the most distinguished designers of the 19th century: the architect Richard Morris Hunt (1828–95) and the landscape architect Frederick Law Olmsted (1822–1903).

Mr. Vanderbilt had known both men for several years; they collaborated on the family mausoleum on Staten Island that William Henry had commissioned in 1884. Hunt, the first American to study at the prestigious Ecole des Beaux-Arts in Paris, was a favorite society architect. He became the unofficial family designer, creating Marble House and The Breakers in Newport, Rhode Island, and a mansion at 660 Fifth Avenue for one of George Vanderbilt's older brothers. Hunt was also responsible for many important public works, such as the main facade of the Metropolitan Museum of Art in New York, the Yorktown Monument in Virginia, and the pedestal for the Statue of Liberty.

Olmsted, who was trained in engineering and agriculture and was known as the founding father of American landscape architecture, had designed scores of parks, most notably New York's Central Park, the U.S. Capitol grounds, and the campus of Stanford University in California. An early conservationist, he also consulted in 1864 on the preservation of Yosemite Valley, which later became one of America's first national parks.

For these gifted professionals, Biltmore represented the pinnacle of their long careers. Together with George Vanderbilt they built not only an estate but also a close working relationship based on cooperation and respect.

BUILDING BEGINS Construction of Biltmore got under way in 1889; it was a massive undertaking that included a mansion, gardens, farms, and woodlands.

The centerpiece was a four-story stone house with a 375-foot-long front facade—a monument that would rival the surrounding mountains in grandeur. Hunt modeled the architecture on the richly ornamented style of the French Renaissance and adapted elements, such as the stair tower and the steeply pitched roof, from three famous early 16th-century châteaux in the Loire Valley: Blois, Chenonceau, and Chambord.

The interiors, too, were inspired by European properties, such as the English country estates of Knole, Hatfield House, and Haddon Hall, which Hunt and his client had visited in 1889 while on a buying trip for furnishings. In turn-of-the-century fashion, Biltmore was to be decorated with custom-made pieces and an eclectic assortment of English, Continental, and American furniture and artworks in a range of period styles.

Biltmore was conceived as a masterwork of design and a marvel of modern technology. In addition to central heating, electricity, and a central plumbing system that piped fresh water from a mountain reservoir several miles away, the House was equipped with fire alarms, mechanical refrigeration, and elevators.

Construction required hundreds of workers—from local laborers who earned 50 cents per day to skilled artisans and internationally known artists. The Viennese sculptor Karl Bitter (1867–1915), a Hunt protégé, was hired to design elaborate works in stone, wood, and bronze. Another noted contributor was the Spanish architect Rafael Guastavino (1842–1908), who emigrated to America in the 1880s and quickly became known for the unique system for building tiled ceiling vaults that he had perfected.

BELOW: *Mr. Vanderbilt bought this photograph of the Château de Blois in 1889, during his trip to the Loire Valley with Hunt. The stair tower of the 16th-century French castle inspired the one at Biltmore, which spirals in the opposite direction.*

TOP LEFT: *Biltmore House was located on a bluff high above the confluence of the French Broad and Swannanoa rivers. In 1889 the site was farmland.* TOP RIGHT: *Building materials and work sheds covered the front court as construction proceeded. The rail line was installed to expedite delivery of supplies.* BOTTOM LEFT: *Scaffolding surrounds the stair tower and entrance door.* BOTTOM RIGHT: *About a thousand masons, carpenters, and other artisans worked on Biltmore House over the course of six years. Seen here are members of the construction crew in 1893.*

Among the countless tons of materials used were limestone hauled 600 miles from Indiana and marble imported from Italy. Supplies were delivered via a three-mile-long private rail spur laid between the depot in a neighboring village and the Estate. An on-site kiln produced some 32,000 bricks daily, and a woodworking factory processed oak and walnut for floors and paneling.

As the House was being built, work also progressed on the grounds. Because the tract had been overworked and the terrain was too "rough" for the extensive parkland George Vanderbilt originally desired, Olmsted devised a more practical plan. He recommended installing a 250-acre pleasure park and a series of gardens around the House, establishing farms along the fertile river bottoms, and replanting the rest of the property as commercial timber forest.

One of Olmsted's first projects was creating a nursery to supply the millions of plants needed for the grounds. In 1890 he hired as nursery superintendent Chauncey Beadle (1867–1950), a Canadian horticulturist trained at Ontario Agricultural College and Cornell University. Beadle remained on the Estate for 60 years, guiding Olmsted's plan to maturity. Gifford Pinchot (1865–1946) was engaged in 1891 to oversee renovation of the forest. An 1889 graduate of Yale University, Pinchot studied forestry at the Ecole Nationale Forestière in Nancy, France, and developed at Biltmore the first planned forestry program in America.

ESTATE LIFE After six years of construction, Biltmore was opened on Christmas Eve 1895, when guests gathered to celebrate with a gaily trimmed tree, holiday feasts, and a coaching party. It was the first of many gala affairs on the Estate, which played host to such luminaries as novelists Edith Wharton and Henry James. Guests also came to relax and partake of a range of diversions, from tennis, archery, and croquet to picnicking, riding, and hunting; evenings brought concerts, parlor games, or perhaps dancing.

Guests could enjoy a range of entertainments, including hiking (above) and picnicking (above right) in the woodlands, playing croquet on the lawn of the Italian Garden (right), or going for a drive in a horse-drawn carriage (far right).

In addition to being used for entertaining, Biltmore was very much a home. It was here that George Vanderbilt started a family and pursued his interests in art, literature, and horticulture. He married American socialite Edith Stuyvesant Dresser (1873–1958) in June 1898 in Paris, and the couple came to live at the Estate that fall after honeymooning in Europe. Their only child, Cornelia (1900–76), was born and grew up at Biltmore.

The Vanderbilts were attended by a large staff, including domestic servants and stable hands, and were known as kind and generous employers. Besides paying good wages and providing comfortable living quarters, they held a Christmas party for the staff each year as a special measure of thanks, decorating an enormous tree with gifts for employees and their children.

As the new century progressed, Mr. Vanderbilt realized his dream of a productive estate. The farms yielded fruits, vegetables, grain crops, meat and dairy products, and honey from 41 beehives. The forest produced some 3,000 cords of firewood annually, which were sold along with lumber processed at Biltmore's own mill. And the 300-acre nursery, complete with greenhouses, cold frames, and seed beds, offered for sale about

FAR LEFT: *Estate employees lined the Approach Road in October 1898 to welcome newlyweds George and Edith Vanderbilt to Biltmore.* LEFT: *Mr. Vanderbilt shows off his daughter Cornelia, born in 1900.* BELOW LEFT: *Cornelia hosts her cousin John Brown at a tea party around 1905.* BELOW: *Edith and Cornelia Vanderbilt lead a parade of carriages through Biltmore Village in 1906.*

five million plants—one of the most complete stocks in the country until it was destroyed by flood in 1916.

George and Edith Vanderbilt were committed to helping others. In 1889, Mr. Vanderbilt purchased the nearby town of Best, renaming it Biltmore Village. Between 1896 and 1902, under Mr. Vanderbilt's direction, the town grew to include a school, hospital, church, shops, and cottages. Constructed primarily to house Estate employees, the cottages were complete with plumbing and central heating, considered unusual amenities for the time. Mr. Vanderbilt also introduced innovative farming techniques to the rural region and championed the founding of the Biltmore Forest School in 1898—the first institute for scientific forestry in America.

In 1901, the Vanderbilts started Biltmore Estate Industries, an apprenticeship program to teach traditional crafts such as woodworking and weaving; students sold their works to earn a living, and often made reproductions of Biltmore furnishings. Two years later, Mrs. Vanderbilt set up the School for Domestic Science, which trained young women in cooking, cleaning, and other housekeeping skills. Students in both programs learned essential skills to expand their job opportunities.

YEARS OF CHANGE While the Vanderbilts owned several other residences, Mr. Vanderbilt was actively involved with the operation of Biltmore until his unexpected death in March 1914 following an emergency appendectomy in Washington, D.C. After his burial in the family mausoleum, in Staten Island, New York, Mrs. Vanderbilt returned to the Estate and resumed her work in the community, becoming the first woman president of the state agricultural society, helping build a new hospital, and advocating literacy programs.

After a time, however, she found managing the large property to be overwhelming and began consolidating her interests. Honoring her husband's wish to preserve Pisgah Forest for the public, she sold nearly 87,000 acres to the federal government in 1915, creating the nucleus of Pisgah National Forest. She sold Biltmore Estate Industries in 1917 and Biltmore Village in 1921; by the late 1920s, the Estate comprised about 11,000 acres (it is currently 8,000 acres).

In 1925, Edith married Senator Peter G. Gerry; the couple maintained homes in Providence, Rhode Island, Washington, D.C., and Asheville. Cornelia continued to live at Biltmore; she had been married the year before at All Souls Church in Biltmore Village to the Honorable John Francis Amherst Cecil (1890–1954),

ABOVE LEFT: *All Souls Church under construction in Biltmore Village.* ABOVE RIGHT. *The first woman president of the North Carolina Agricultural Society, Edith Vanderbilt takes the wheel of a tractor as Cornelia looks on.* BELOW: *Cornelia and John Cecil with their first child, George. Both of their sons were born at Biltmore Estate.*

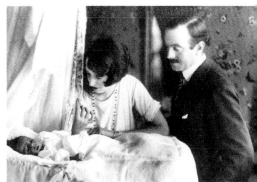

a descendant of William Cecil (1520–98), Lord Burghley, who was Lord High Treasurer to Queen Elizabeth I. Their two sons, George Henry Vanderbilt Cecil and William Amherst Vanderbilt Cecil, were born on the Estate in 1925 and 1928, respectively.

Biltmore continued to serve the region, just as it had in Mr. Vanderbilt's day. Acting on a request by the city of Asheville, which hoped to revitalize the Depression-era economy with tourism, the Cecils opened the Estate to the public for the first time in March 1930. During World War II, when it was believed the capital was at risk of air attack, priceless artworks from the National Gallery of Art were sent to the House for safekeeping. During this time the Biltmore dairy grew into a thriving enterprise that provided both employment and top-quality products.

BELOW: Biltmore's textile conservators repair one of the eight 16th-century tapestries collected by Mr. Vanderbilt.

BILTMORE TODAY In 1960, William Cecil left a banking career in New York City and Washington, D.C., to join his brother in managing Biltmore, which they inherited under the terms of a trust. His goal was not only to return the historic site to its turn-of-the-century splendor but also to perpetuate his grandfather's ideal of self-sufficiency.

Under Mr. Cecil's stewardship, more than 90 rooms, with thousands of original objects, were opened to the public. He also began an ongoing preservation program, which makes it possible to experience the Estate as it was during the Vanderbilts' residence. Mrs. Vanderbilt's Bedroom, for instance, was restored in 1990 using reproductions of the original French fabrics—woven on the same looms used a century earlier. In the Library, conservators removed, restored, and reinstalled the 2,000-square-foot ceiling painting. Biltmore's expert textile conservators today continue the complex project of cleaning and repairing the eight 16th-century Flemish tapestries in the collection.

Mr. Cecil also brought changes to Biltmore to keep it a self-sufficient landmark. After the dairy, under the leadership of George Cecil, became a separate business in 1979, the dairy barn was remodeled for use as a winery, which has become the most

ABOVE: *Autumn vistas extend for miles from the Biltmore House Loggia.*

visited wine-making facility in America. Angus and Limousin beef cattle have been introduced in the farm operation, and a breeding program has produced several champions. And each winter, *Candlelight Christmas Evenings*, featuring nearly 40 decorated trees inside Biltmore House, rekindle the festive spirit of a Gilded Age holiday.

Today, William Cecil's son, William A.V. Cecil, Jr., serves as CEO of Biltmore Estate. He continues the preservation efforts begun by his father, and focuses on ensuring that Biltmore Estate lives up to the standards established by his great-grandfather more than a century ago. In keeping with George Vanderbilt's vision, Biltmore is entirely self-sustaining, receiving neither government subsidies nor private grants. Its operations and preservation efforts are supported by a variety of ventures, including guest admissions, selective timber harvesting, restaurants and shops, and collections of finely crafted Biltmore Estate reproductions. The Estate, with a staff of 1,000, also contributes to the community as one of the region's largest employers.

Most importantly, Biltmore today maintains the tradition of hospitality engendered by its founder, welcoming more than 900,000 guests each year. Named a National Historic Landmark in 1963, Biltmore continues to attract visitors to its celebrated house and gardens, and to inspire all who see it just as it has since 1895.

Biltmore House

No residence in America brings the glorious Gilded Age more vividly to life than Biltmore House. Faithfully preserved and filled with thousands of original furnishings, its rooms suggest that the Vanderbilts are still at home. From opulent living quarters enjoyed by family and friends to the "downstairs" domain of the domestic staff, the House presents a detailed portrait of a great 19th-century country estate.

*O*N THE MAIN FLOOR OF BILTMORE ARE THE PUBLIC rooms in which the Vanderbilts lived as a family and entertained their guests. Arranged around a light-filled garden court are an entry hall, a game room, and several dining and sitting areas; set off by itself is an expansive library, a quiet retreat for study or solitude. The decor throughout is richly elegant, reflecting the traditions of European country estates.

ENTRANCE HALL With its soaring limestone arches and polished marble floor, the Entrance Hall is an impressive introduction to Biltmore House. Its focal point is a massive oak table designed by Richard Morris Hunt, which displays a group of bronzes by renowned French artist Antoine-Louis Barye (1796–1875). Inspired by the 16th-century Italian epic poem *Orlando Furioso*, the center sculpture portrays the hero, Roger, rescuing his love, Angelique, on a mythical creature called the Hippogriff. The flanking candelabra are modeled with figures of Roman goddesses Juno, Minerva, and Venus.

WINTER GARDEN Glass-roofed garden rooms were considered quite stylish in the Victorian era, providing a place to relax or entertain amid an indoor "jungle" of exotic plants. Rattan and bamboo furniture such as this suite bought by Mr. Vanderbilt in France was fashionable for garden use. The central element of this indoor garden setting is a marble and bronze fountain sculpture, *Boy Stealing Geese*, by Karl Bitter, a Viennese artist who emigrated to America in 1889.

The adjoining corridor features tiled ceiling vaults designed by the Spanish architect Rafael Guastavino. On the walls are plaster copies of sections of the Elgin Marbles, crafted in the 1890s by French artist Eugene Arrondelle. The originals once adorned the Parthenon in Athens and are now housed in the British Museum.

ABOVE: *Preserved in the pages of the Nonsense Book, a type of scrapbook for Biltmore's guests, is a sketch drawn in 1902 of Karl Bitter's bronze figures.* RIGHT: *Cornelia Vanderbilt and John Cecil held their wedding breakfast by the fountain in 1924.* OPPOSITE: *At Christmastime the palms, ficus, and other tropical plants in the Winter Garden are enhanced by colorful poinsettias.*

BILLIARD ROOM Part of a series of rooms known as the Bachelors' Wing, the Billiard Room provided a retreat for the Vanderbilts' male guests. (Concealed doors on either side of the fireplace lead to other rooms in the wing.) Although female guests were welcome, the room was primarily a place where men could enjoy each other's company and indulge in billiards, played on the carom table (with no pockets), or pool, played on the pool table (with six pockets). Both games became so popular by the late 18th century that special rooms like this began to appear in country homes.

The Billiard Room resembles exclusive gentlemen's social clubs of the age—with rich oak paneling, an ornamental plaster ceiling, and deep-hued Oriental carpets. Equally masculine are the leather settees and armchairs made in London in 1895; the pieces are reproductions of 17th-century furniture from Knole, an English estate that Mr. Vanderbilt and Hunt visited in 1889.

Displayed around the room are examples from Mr. Vanderbilt's print collection. Many of the works are based on paintings by the British artists Sir Joshua Reynolds (1723–92), George Stubbs (1724–1806), and Sir Edwin Landseer (1802–73). Above the sofa is the painting *Rosita* by Ignacio Zuloaga y Zaboleta (1870–1945), a highly regarded Spanish genre and portrait painter.

OPPOSITE: *Illuminated by wrought-iron light fixtures made especially for the room, the American oak game tables are each topped with three slabs of slate weighing about 900 pounds. Many of the 24 cue sticks, stored in their original oak stands, are inlaid with ivory and mother-of-pearl.*

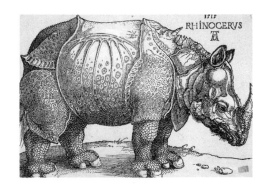

Prints

Mr. Vanderbilt was an avid collector of prints, acquiring about 1,600 etchings, woodcuts, aquatints, photogravures, and other printed works throughout his life. Examples from the collection, which includes sporting, architecture, landscape, still-life, and portrait prints, are (clockwise from above left) Rhinocerus, *a 1515 woodcut by Albrecht Dürer; a likeness of Cardinal Richelieu engraved in 1657 by Robert Nanteuil; and* Chartres: Street Scene and Cathedral, *an 1882 etching by Axel Haig.*

BANQUET HALL As imposing as a great hall in a medieval castle, the Banquet Hall is the largest room in the House, measuring 72 feet long by 42 feet wide with a 70-foot-high barrel-vaulted ceiling. It was in this baronial space that the Vanderbilts entertained formally, hosted birthday parties for Cornelia, and held their annual Christmas festivities—a tradition that continues to this day.

Because of the room's vast dimensions, Hunt designed special furniture for it, including two built-in gilt-trimmed throne chairs, an oak dining table, and 64 chairs. The architect also created a suitable setting for the five Flemish tapestries that Mr. Vanderbilt is thought to have purchased in Paris in 1887. These intricate textiles, woven of silk, wool, and metallic thread between 1546 and 1553, are part of an original set of seven portraying the story from Roman mythology of Venus (goddess of love); her paramour, Mars (god of war); and her jealous husband, Vulcan (god of fire).

The triple fireplace, flanked with armor dating from the 1400s to 1800s, features on its overmantel a high-relief panel entitled *The Return from the Chase.* It was carved by Bitter, who was also responsible for the oak mural on the organ gallery. Although an instrument was not originally installed, an organ from the period has been restored and placed in the room. Below the gallery is a built-in sideboard showcasing a collection of 18th- and 19th-century brass and copper vessels from Holland, France, and Spain.

The pennants hanging in the room include the Biltmore Estate service flag, commemorating staff members who fought in World War I, and replicas of flags from the American Revolution and the 13 original colonies. Those hanging above the fireplace represent countries in power when Christopher Columbus sailed to North America; the 400th anniversary of his second voyage was celebrated in 1893 by the World's Columbian Exposition in Chicago, which Mr. Vanderbilt visited.

ABOVE: *Each of the hundreds of pieces in the family table service bears a monogram; this tureen is marked with "CSV" for Cornelia Stuyvesant Vanderbilt.* OPPOSITE: *As part of the complete restoration of the Breakfast Room in 1993, the seating furniture was reupholstered and the draperies replaced using 350 yards of silk cut velvet matched to the original pattern. The fabric was woven by Tassinari & Chatel of Lyons, France—the same textile firm that filled Mr. Vanderbilt's order in the 1890s.*

BREAKFAST ROOM Designed on a more intimate scale than the Banquet Hall, this room was intended for less formal dining and was probably used for all three meals. Nevertheless, the room is elegant, with Italian marble wainscoting and door trim, a tooled-leather wall covering, and a fireplace surround of Wedgwood-style jasperware tiles. The ornate plasterwork ceiling is highlighted with a gold-tinted glaze and features heavy pendants that terminate in tiny acorns—one of the symbols in the Vanderbilt family crest.

No finery was spared in setting the dining table, spread with damask linens probably woven in Ireland and embroidered in Paris. Seated on gilt-legged chairs with cut-velvet upholstery, diners were served their meals on gold-trimmed porcelain dinnerware made by Minton, the noted Staffordshire ceramics manufacturer. And, they drank from crystal glasses—etched with Vanderbilt monograms—produced by Baccarat of France and Thomas Webb and Sons of England.

Among the family portraits in this room are likenesses of Mr. Vanderbilt's father, William Henry, located above the display case, and of his mother, Maria Louisa, to the right of the fireplace. There are two paintings of his grandfather, Cornelius: the circa 1839 portrait to the left of the fireplace shows him as a young man (appropriately, for a mariner, holding a spyglass) and the circa 1876 portrait above the Banquet Hall door depicts him as a successful businessman.

SALON Just as the men of the household adjourned to the Billiard Room, women would retire to the Salon for conversation or reading; they might even step out on the adjoining balcony to take some air and view the landscape. The decor features graceful French furniture, including 19th-century Louis XV-style seating furniture with their original tapestry-weave upholstery and a folding screen with petit-point panels. The room is also a showcase for prints by Albrecht Dürer (1471–1528), the noted artist of the Northern Renaissance, and prints of châteaux in the Loire Valley.

At each end of the room are hangings made for Cardinal Richelieu, the 17th-century French statesman; such hangings were used in the 1600s as decoration behind the chairs of high-ranking officials. Stitched with embroidery and metal-thread couching, the velvet textiles depict his armorial bearings, cardinal's hat, and Latin motto, *Semper Idem* ("always the same").

Reflecting Mr. Vanderbilt's interest in the Napoleonic era is the Empire walnut game table and ivory chess pieces owned and used by Napoleon Bonaparte during his exile on St. Helena island between 1815 and 1821. After the deposed emperor's death, his heart was placed in a silver urn on the table before being put into his coffin.

Games

At Biltmore, family and guests had a choice of pleasant pastimes, from cribbage to checkers. Card games, such as whist and euchre, were played with gaily decorated decks (top). Chess players used a 19th-century game table and ivory pieces (above left) originally owned by Napoleon Bonaparte. Gentlemen gambled with poker chips and an American-made walnut roulette wheel (above right). Mah-jongg was a popular Chinese game using tiles, and Biltmore's set (right)—made in Hong Kong—is located in the Second Floor Living Hall.

MUSIC ROOM Plans for Biltmore indicate that a music room was intended for this location, although it remained unfinished for 81 years. What had been an empty space with bare brick walls was completed and opened in 1976. The room is decorated to reflect the French Renaissance style and includes wall paneling carved of red oak harvested from Biltmore's forest and polychrome painting on the boxed ceiling beams.

The room was also designed to display several treasures. The fireplace mantel, designed by Hunt and carved with Albrecht Dürer's initials and life dates, was found below the stables prior to installation in the Music Room. Above it hangs a late 18th-century printing of the woodcut known as the *Triumphal Arch*, which Holy

Roman Emperor Maximilian I (1459–1519) commissioned from Dürer and others around 1515. Measuring about 10 feet tall by 10 feet wide, the work depicts military and political events, references to the emperor's prowess as a hunter and linguist, and a family tree with mythological and human characters.

On the shelves beside the print is a rare collection of 12 apostle figures and 12 candlesticks. Based on statuary in the Basilica of St. John Lateran in Rome, the gilt-trimmed porcelain sculptures are the work of Johann Joachim Kändler (1706–75), master modeler at the Meissen factory near Dresden. The pieces came from several different sets made between 1735 and 1741 for Empresses Amalia and Maria Theresa of the Austrian Hapsburgs.

INSET, ABOVE: *The figure of St. Matthew is part of a set portraying the 12 apostles that was produced by the Meissen porcelain factory in the mid-1700s. The base is marked with the Austrian imperial crest; the Biltmore sculptures are based* on statuary found in a Roman basilica. BELOW: *A detail from the monumental Triumphal Arch, designed by Albrecht Dürer and others.* Comprising 192 separately printed blocks, the work arrived at Biltmore just before Christmas 1895, shipped by train in three boxes. OPPOSITE: *Unfinished during Mr. Vanderbilt's lifetime, the Music Room contains a Steinway piano — played by Van Cliburn during his visit to the Estate in 1961 — and an elaborately carved and gilded 18th-century music stand.*

TAPESTRY GALLERY Opening off the Entrance Hall, this 90-foot-long room served as a sitting area and perhaps a ballroom. The space was also designed to display three silk-and-wool

tapestries woven in Brussels around 1530. Part of an original set of seven known as *The Triumph of the Seven Virtues*, the pieces are distinguished by richly detailed pictorial designs that personify Prudence, Faith, and Charity and incorporate biblical, mythological, and historical images.

Other notable furnishings include three 19th-century Persian rugs—examples of the several hundred Eastern carpets Mr. Vanderbilt acquired on his trips to Europe. A receipt from 1889 reveals that he bought 300 carpets at one time from one London dealer. Not all the furniture, however, came from abroad. The two gateleg tables with spiral-twist legs were probably produced by Biltmore Estate Industries, the handicraft program founded by the Vanderbilts in 1901.

Three family portraits hang on the paneled wall to the Library. Over the door is the likeness of George Vanderbilt, painted in 1895, and to the left is that of his mother, Maria Louisa Kissam Vanderbilt, painted around 1888. Both are the work of John Singer Sargent (1856–1925), one of the most celebrated society portraitists of his time. On the right is Edith Vanderbilt by Giovanni Boldini (1842–1931), an Italian artist who enjoyed an international reputation at the turn of the century. On the opposite wall, near the entrance hall, is another portrait of Edith Vanderbilt. Entitled *Ivory and Gold*, it was painted in 1902 by James Abbott McNeill Whistler (1834–1903), the famous expatriate American artist.

LEFT: *Providing a colorful setting for three 16th-century Flemish tapestries are stenciled ceiling beams and painted limestone fireplace hoods modeled after those in the Château de Pierrefonds near Compiègne, France.*
ABOVE: *One of three fearsome serpent heads, part of the complex design of the Triumph of Prudence tapestry, is shown in detail.*

LIBRARY Of all the rooms in Biltmore House, the Library best reflects Mr. Vanderbilt's intellect and personality. An avid reader and book lover from childhood, George Vanderbilt began acquiring books by age 11. He amassed a collection of more than 23,000 volumes in eight languages, about 10,000 of which are housed in the Library's walnut stacks. His interests were wide-ranging, as evidenced by books on everything from architecture to agriculture.

Mr. Vanderbilt enjoyed sharing his library with guests. A passage behind the mantel leads to the second floor, which provided easy access for guests to select volumes for bedtime reading. (Even so, Henry James, the noted American author who visited Biltmore in 1905, complained that his bedroom was at least half a mile away from the "mile-long library.")

Among the striking features of the room is a dramatic ceiling painting—*The Chariot of Aurora*, by the Venetian artist Giovanni Antonio Pellegrini (1675–1741). Originally located in the ballroom of the Pisani Palace in Venice, the work comprises 13 separate canvases and measures about 64 feet long by 32 feet wide.

Equally impressive are the black marble fireplace surround and the walnut overmantel, both carved by Bitter. Baroque-style carvings and female figures flank the 17th-century French tapestry. In 1999–2000, upholstery, drapery fabric, and trims were painstakingly reproduced to restore the Library to its original appearance.

OPPOSITE: *Stocked with books dating as early as 1561, the Library was a source of both recreation and information for its scholarly owner, who employed a librarian to catalog his 23,000-volume collection.*

ABOVE LEFT: *Making the room appear open to the sky, the ceiling painting represents dawn. It is one of the most important canvases by Pellegrini extant, as many of his works were destroyed in the world wars.*

ABOVE RIGHT: *In this circa 1898 photograph, Cedric, one of the family's St. Bernards, rests in front of an ornate reading table designed by Hunt.*

*W*HEREAS THE FIRST FLOOR HOUSED THE GRAND PUBLIC ROOMS, the second story was home to the Vanderbilts' private quarters and a series of guest suites. The floor is organized around a central sitting area where men and women could socialize, read, write letters, and play games. This and two other upper floors were reached by either a staircase or an Otis elevator, which traveled 100 feet per minute and was the first passenger elevator in Asheville.

LOUIS XVI ROOM One of 32 guest rooms at Biltmore—needed to accommodate the Vanderbilts' large house parties—the Louis XVI Room exemplifies the rage for French decorating styles in the late 19th century. The room is characterized by its oval shape and its location above the main entrance to Biltmore House.

Decorated in neo-classical Louis XVI style—popular in the third quarter of the 18th century—the room is named for the King of France at that time. The style is represented by delicate column-shaped furniture legs, floral swags, and other classical Greek and Roman motifs.

Reflecting this style are the French-made *chaise longue*, side chairs, and center table—all Louis XVI revival pieces with slender, reeded legs and delicate swag or scroll motifs. Red damask upholstery and wall covering similar to the original, as well as lightly patterned Aubusson carpets, contribute to the refined look of the oval room.

Pauline Merrill, Edith Vanderbilt's sister, described in a letter her experience while staying in this room as a guest in 1905. *"I breakfast in my room which is oval shape...the walls hung in old crimson brocade & all the furniture & decorations Louis XVI..."*

ABOVE LEFT: *The 102-step Grand Staircase stretches to the fourth floor. Running through its center is a large wrought-iron chandelier illuminated by 72 electric bulbs and suspended from a single point.*

ABOVE RIGHT: *This cartel clock is French, ca. 1760, made by Louis Jouard of Paris in the Louis XV style. The case is gilt brass with an enameled and painted dial. It is an eight-day time and strike clock which chimed on the hour and half hour. "Cartel" indicates the clock was designed to be attached to a wall, mirror, or other flat vertical surface. Cartel clocks were generally round or oval with pointed, elongated ends.* OPPOSITE: *The Louis XVI Room is one of several bedrooms designed in an oval, which was in vogue for interiors in 18th-century France. The shape and size of this room seem to dwarf the bed, which is, in fact, a six-foot-long double bed.*

SECOND FLOOR LIVING HALL The Living Hall was an informal area where occupants of the second-floor guest rooms, along with family members, could mingle before meals or spend a lazy afternoon reading or chatting. Upholstered furniture in intimate groupings invited conversation, while a handsome Boulle-style desk offered a perfect place for letter writing.

Today the room serves as a gallery for several important paintings. In prominent positions on the north wall are full-length portraits of the two architects who helped translate Mr. Vanderbilt's vision for the Estate into reality. On the right is a portrait of Frederick Law Olmsted; the landscape designer is fittingly shown in a woodland setting beside a blossoming rhododendron. On the left is a portrait of Richard Morris Hunt, who is posed in front of the outside stair tower (although the weather was so chilly when the portrait was made that he actually

stood indoors by a fireplace). Both were painted by John Singer Sargent, who came to Biltmore in May 1895 to capture these men on canvas. Between them hangs *The Waltz* by Anders Zorn (1860–1920), the respected Swedish artist; Mr. Vanderbilt purchased the painting in 1893 at the World's Columbian Exposition in Chicago, where it was on exhibit.

Family portraits include a likeness of Cornelia Vanderbilt Cecil, painted in the 1920s by the Russian artist Nikol Schattenstein (1877–1955). The group portrait at the east end is of the William Cecil family, painted by the prominent New York artist and Asheville native Stone Roberts (1951–). At the opposite end hangs *Going to the Opera—Family Portrait*, depicting the William Henry Vanderbilt family in 1873, by the American painter Seymour Guy (1824–75); 11-year-old George Vanderbilt is seated at the table.

OPPOSITE: *The two tones of brown on the walls of the Living Hall are terra cotta and coffee brown. Through paint analysis these colors were carefully chosen to match the originals. This color scheme is found throughout the House in family and guest areas.*

Clocks

Among the most intricate and varied objects at Biltmore are the clocks—from the tall-case clock in the Entrance Hall to the massive tower clock on the Stable to the mirror-mounted cartel clock in the Louis XVI Room. The 19 timepieces displayed from the collection range from the mid-17th century to the early 20th century and were made primarily in England and France. Shown here are a circa 1780 arch-top bracket clock (far left) by Coward and Company, a gilt-and-bronze statue clock (top left) with works by Japy Frères from around 1870, and an inverted basket-top bracket clock (bottom left) made by Edmund Card in the late 1600s.

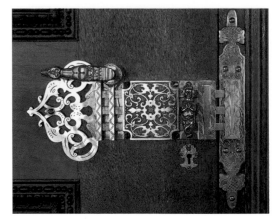

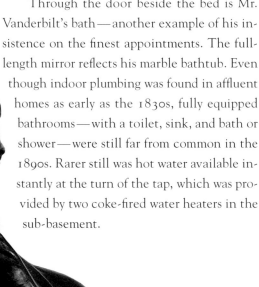

TOP LEFT: *No detail in the bedroom was overlooked: the elaborate brass door latch was hand cast with floral and figural elements.* TOP RIGHT: *Mr. Vanderbilt's bathroom, plumbed with hot and cold running water, features a paw-footed tub.* RIGHT: *The bronze bust of Mr. Vanderbilt was created by the Scottish artist Mary Grant in 1889; it is displayed in the Library.* OPPOSITE: *Befitting the head of the household is this dignified room, with deep ceiling moldings and a gilded wall covering. The furniture is a mixture of Baroque-style pieces from the 17th and 19th centuries. Mr. Vanderbilt's bed is a fine example of the intricate turned and carved walnut furniture produced in 17th-century Portugal.*

MR. VANDERBILT'S BEDROOM The owner of Biltmore was a man accustomed to the best, and he settled for nothing less in siting and furnishing his bedroom. It is located in the southwest corner of the House, where he could enjoy a commanding view of his property—from the wooded deer park below to Mount Pisgah, 17 miles in the distance. The room is filled with heavily carved and turned walnut pieces, including a dressing table, *chaise longue*, and chairs designed by Hunt and inspired by the grand Baroque style.

Mr. Vanderbilt surrounded himself with the art objects he loved, such as fine engravings by 16th- and 17th-century artists from Germany and Holland and bronze sculptures from 19th-century France.

Through the door beside the bed is Mr. Vanderbilt's bath—another example of his insistence on the finest appointments. The full-length mirror reflects his marble bathtub. Even though indoor plumbing was found in affluent homes as early as the 1830s, fully equipped bathrooms—with a toilet, sink, and bath or shower—were still far from common in the 1890s. Rarer still was hot water available instantly at the turn of the tap, which was provided by two coke-fired water heaters in the sub-basement.

OAK SITTING ROOM Connecting Mr. and Mrs. Vanderbilt's private quarters, this well-appointed room was used as a private sitting area for the couple. The ornate architectural detailing recalls the Jacobean splendor of the Great Hall at Hatfield House, a 17th-century English estate that Mr. Vanderbilt visited with Hunt during their trip to Europe in 1889. The plaster ceiling is webbed with intricate strapwork, the cornice frieze is marked with repeating coats of arms, and the walls are clad with exquisitely carved oak paneling.

The setting is complemented by the stately furnishings, which include several remarkable case pieces. In the corner is a carved ebony cabinet-on-stand made in Antwerp in the 1600s with parquetry doors that open to reveal a classically inspired architectural scene. Resembling a miniature loggia, it is decorated with a patterned floor, marbleized columns, and gilt-trimmed statuary overlooking a trompe-l'oeil landscape painting.

The room also features two portraits by Sargent. On the right, in a black dress, is *Virginia Purdy Bacon*, a cousin and close friend of Mr. Vanderbilt's; on the left is *Mrs. Benjamin Kissam*, his aunt.

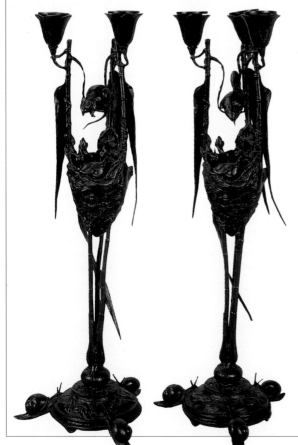

Bronzes

Of the more than 40 bronze sculptures on display at Biltmore, about half are pieces created by les Animaliers—a 19th-century French school of art so called because its adherents specialized in naturalistic depictions of animals. The most well-known of the group was Antoine-Louis Barye, who is considered one of the finest animal sculptors in history. Mr. Vanderbilt had seen Barye's work in Paris and acquired a number of his sculptures, including the striking Hippogriff seen in the Entrance Hall. Throughout the House are also pieces by Pierre-Jules Mène, whose stag (above left) exemplifies the artist's skill in portraying a moment of an animal's life in the wild; August Nicholas Cain, who crafted these candlesticks (left) ornamented with bird nests; and Jean-François-Théodore Gechter, who was known for his horse figures, such as this horse spooked by a snake (below).

MRS. VANDERBILT'S BEDROOM This graceful, feminine room was designed as a counterpart to Mr. Vanderbilt's Bedroom. When he was still a bachelor, the room was used by his mother, Maria Louisa Kissam Vanderbilt, during her visits to the Estate. After his marriage, it became the private quarters of Edith Stuyvesant Dresser Vanderbilt.

Like her husband, Edith Vanderbilt was a member of a prominent family. Among her ancestors were Peter Stuyvesant, the first governor of Dutch colonial New York in the mid-17th century, and several respected senators, judges, and mayors. Orphaned at the age of ten, Edith Dresser and her sisters were raised by their maternal grandmother in Newport, Rhode Island. According to contemporary accounts, she was considered "a very charming young lady" and "the perfection of hostesses."

Her courtship with George Vanderbilt began in Paris in 1896; they had already known one another for several years. Engaged in April 1898, the couple wed in June in a simple ceremony, attended by 150 family members and friends, at the American Cathedral in Paris.

When they arrived at the Estate in October, after their honeymoon in Europe, Mrs. Vanderbilt saw her room just as it appears today. The oval-shaped space is decorated in the Louis XV style, originated in France around 1700 and adopted by affluent Americans in the late 1800s. The room incorporates such hallmarks of this luxurious style as silk wall covering, fancily trimmed mirrors, Savonnerie carpets, and cut-velvet draperies on the windows and bed. The two marble-topped commodes are French period pieces; the chairs and chaise are in the Louis XV Revival style, typified by white frames, carved floral motifs, and curving profiles. Complementing the look is a collection of French and German prints from the 18th century and a Louis XV clock elaborately embellished with porcelain figurines and flowers, believed to be Phillipe Barat's masterpiece, earning him entry into the French Clockmaker's guild in 1764.

OPPOSITE: *The sumptuous cut velvet used for the draperies and upholstery in Mrs. Vanderbilt's Bedroom is a duplicate of the original fabric. It was woven for the restoration of the room in 1990 by Tassinari & Chatel, which retained the loom pattern from which the material had been made a century ago.* LEFT ABOVE: *A charming, fashionable woman, Mrs. Vanderbilt was the gracious hostess of Biltmore.* LEFT BELOW: *Mrs. Vanderbilt was a devoted mother to her only daughter, Cornelia, seen here around age 5, who often accompanied her on weekly visits to families living on the Estate.*

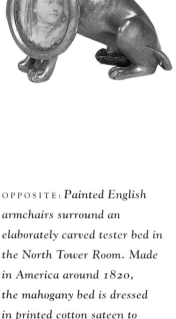

*L*IKE THE SECOND FLOOR, THE THIRD FLOOR FEAtures a number of spacious guest rooms—each one decorated in a different style, as was fashionable in the late 19th century—and also includes a centrally located sitting area. The rooms here were removed from the noise and bustle of the first floor and occupied by guests whose names were written on small cards posted on each door—lest visitors lose their way among the many bedrooms on this level.

NORTH TOWER ROOM These elegant guest quarters are part of a suite of four interconnected rooms opened in April 1995 after two years of exhaustive research and restoration. Given their grand size and prominent location—directly above the Vanderbilts' own bedrooms and sitting area—the guest rooms probably were among the most elaborate in the house. The suite could have been shared by a family or groups of guests visiting together.

The North Tower Room, shaped in a graceful oval, is decorated in a mixture of styles from the late 18th and early 19th centuries. Furnishings include the 19th-century balloon clock, the delicate armchairs, with their attenuated frame and painted finish, and the languorous *chaise longue*, whose lions-paw feet are modeled on a classical motif.

EARLOM ROOM This room was inspired by nine prints in Mr. Vanderbilt's collection from the English engraver Richard Earlom (1745–1822). Centerpieces among the eclectic array of furnishings are an armoire and a fall-front bombé bureau—both mid-18th-century examples of Dutch cabinetmakers' command of exacting marquetry decoration. The silk-screened, two-toned wallpaper is an exact reproduction of the original, and the cotton cut velvet used for the upholstery, bedspread, and draperies was reproduced from fabric found on the suite of five Spanish Revival chairs placed around the room.

OPPOSITE: *Painted English armchairs surround an elaborately carved tester bed in the North Tower Room. Made in America around 1820, the mahogany bed is dressed in printed cotton sateen to match the wall covering and upholstery—all reproductions of the fabric found in the room before restoration.* ABOVE: *This little gilded bulldog, its leash clenched in its mouth, wears a "tag" bearing a photograph of Lila Vanderbilt taken around 1863; it was made by Tiffany and Co. in the mid-19th century.* LEFT: *Period designers recommended that bedrooms display colors of "medium scale" and "delicate contrast." The Earlom Room features warm, neutral shades, as seen in the terra-cotta wallpaper and ivory and olive green paint.*

RAPHAEL ROOM As in the Earlom Room, the Raphael Room was designed around a series of prints—in this case 18th- and 19th-century engravings after paintings by the Renaissance master Raphael Sanzio (1483–1520). The 14 artworks, which were executed by several European printmakers, depict the range of subjects for which Raphael is famous, including images of the Madonna and the Holy Family and figures from Christianity and classical mythology.

In contrast to the intricate engravings is the room's understated decor. The wallpaper displays a subtle pattern, the English and American 19th-century furniture boasts little ornamentation beyond its mahogany veneer, and the fabric is a plain cotton velveteen. The simple, refined appearance of this bedroom reflects both the late-19th-century trend toward less cluttered interiors—a reaction against the excessive opulence of the mid-Victorian era—and the restrained style that arbiters of taste considered appropriate for country retreats.

INSET, RIGHT: This diminutive railcar, complete with couplers and curtains, was made by the French cristallerie Baccarat around 1890 as a carriage for perfume flasks; the cushions at each end were designed for storing hat pins. BELOW: Crafted in France in the 19th century, this ornate miniature furniture measuring only four inches tall is hand painted with pastoral scenes.

SOUTH TOWER ROOM Pastel colors and dainty floral-printed fabric mark the South Tower Room, a large, round space decorated in a subdued neoclassical style. The striated wallpaper was adapted from a pattern by William Morris (1834–96), a leading English proponent of "aesthetic" handcrafted design, and is complemented by mauve and ivory trim—the original woodwork colors, which were discovered under a subsequent layer of paint.

Much of the furniture, such as the white bed with caned head- and footboards, the center table, the inlaid commode, and the painted table, are from late-19th-century France. The remaining pieces, including a suite of Cuban mahogany ballroom chairs, were made primarily in England between the late 1700s and early 1900s. In addition to the blue satin covering the sidechair and seat cushions, a striped cotton fabric was used for the draperies, bed furnishings, and upholstery; it was reproduced from the original fabric on the tufted sofa.

THIRD FLOOR LIVING HALL The primary "living room" for the upper guest wing, the Third Floor Living Hall was intended for relaxing and socializing. Houseguests could take tea, match wits over parlor games, curl up with a book, or listen to the player piano.

ABOVE: *The blue-and-yellow color scheme of the Raphael Room was popular in the 19th century, with blue especially favored to complement the ruddy tones of mahogany, seen here in the sleigh bed and cupboard secretary.*
LEFT: *Indicative of the attention paid to every detail during renovation is the variety of textile trims used in the South Tower Room. Four different types of fringe and 40 tassels were chosen to coordinate with the satin and cotton fabrics.*

FOUR UNIQUE BEDROOMS, CALLED THE ARTISTS' SUITE, were restored and opened to the public in 1999. Located off the Third Floor Living Hall, each guest room was named on original Biltmore House plans after artists or works of art. Each is restored to a different furnishing style, depending on the artist or works of art featured and the clues provided by original wall coverings and other evidence in the rooms.

ABOVE: *This unusual vase, by the famed art glass maker Louis Comfort Tiffany, demonstrates his mastery of glassmaking techniques. The hand-blown vase features different layers of glass in different colors, with a gold metallic surface and woven sterling silver overlay.*

WATSON ROOM Named after the 18th-century engraver James Watson (1740–1790), the room reflects the English artist's refined neoclassical style. Watson was the favorite engraver of the famous 18th-century portraitist Sir Joshua Reynolds, and George Vanderbilt amassed a large collection of his mezzotints, many of which are on display throughout the room.

The furniture, including a set of mahogany and boxwood twin beds from England, the only twin beds in the Biltmore collection, showcases classical details such as urn shapes and delicate straight legs. A vivid pattern of purple irises and multicolored flowers is featured on the room's dominant fabric, reproduced from an original late-19th-century textile. This same fabric was found to have been used in a pair of drapery panels and as upholstered seats for the room's two neoclassical side chairs. Both the colors of the fabric and of the room's trim, painted to match the original, coordinate with the fireplace's marble surround. The inkstand on the tambour-top desk is an exquisite combination of early-19th-century Chinese porcelain parts and late-19th-century French gilt bronze. The glass Tiffany vase with silver webbing on the center of the table dates to 1890.

VAN DYCK ROOM Anthony Van Dyck (1599–1641) was a prominent 17th-century Dutch painter, and prints of his still-famous portraits adorn this eclectic room, furnished primarily according to a Colonial Revival motif, a style widely used in turn-of-the-century interiors.

The deep green trim and terra-cotta and tan floral wallpaper complement an assortment of 19th-century furniture, including a mahogany chest-on-cabinet in the style of George III, which features painted scenes inspired by Swiss painter Angelica Kauffman (1741–1807), and a decoratively carved walnut bed in the French Empire style. Fabric reproduced from an original in the Biltmore Estate textile collection was used to cover the room's *chaise longue*, which is equipped with a silver pull at the rear that allows the piece to recline. The window seat offered guests a place for respite, along with a panoramic view of the deer park.

Complementing the room's trim, the fireplace mantel's two shades of original green paint were conserved and stabilized as an example of turn-of-the-century decorative painting technique. Objects from the 1700s, 1800s, and early 1900s decorate the room, including two 18th-century German ceramic figurines. George Vanderbilt inherited the pair of Japanese Satsuma-ware porcelain vases, painted with parades of realistic insects, from the large art collection of his father, William H. Vanderbilt.

BELOW: *The canopy fabric was hand-painted by an accomplished artist who spent months reproducing it from the original. The original panels were most likely made for export to Persia, then purchased many decades later by Vanderbilt.*

MORLAND ROOM Exotic and Rococo Revival influences make the Morland Room, named after popular genre painter George Morland (1762/3–1804), both unusual and elegant. The focus of the room is the bed canopy, with drapery panels decorated with lively animals, flowers, and hunting scenes. The hand-painted fabric is a careful reproduction of the early-19th-century Indian chintz originally used in this room. Before they arrived at Biltmore, the original fabric panels were hung on the dining room walls of the honeymoon cottage George and Edith Vanderbilt rented in Stressa, Italy.

The oak and linen daybed and arm chair of the Morland Room are covered in coordinating fabric of exotic birds, flowers, and foliage in shades of blue and red. All are highlighted by the light turquoise damask pattern and shimmering silver ground of the room's wallpaper. Scraps of the original wallpaper were found behind light fixtures, then matched to several rolls of the paper still in storage, allowing an exact reproduction to be made.

In addition to the Indian textiles, many decorative objects in the room are in keeping with the 19th-century movement known as *exoticism*, a fascination with imported items from countries such as India and China. The brilliant jade tree decorating the mantel was made in China in the early 20th century of turquoise, coral, enamel, metal, and other materials. From the same period in China are the glazed ceramic parrot figurines. The porcelain tea caddy is from early-19th-century China, and the ceramic, wood, and brass lamp was created in the early 20th century from a Chinese vase.

MADONNA ROOM Prints after masterpieces of the Italian Renaissance, including works by Titian and Raphael, illustrate the theme of the Madonna Room and reflect its Renaissance revival style. A reproduction of the original, the room's wallpaper imitates the look of a 15th-century textile woven with fine gold threads. This shimmering effect is repeated in the gold fabric, roping, and brush fringe used on the room's drapery and upholstery, all of which are identical to the originals.

The room features finely carved Italian-style furniture. At the foot of the bed is a *cassone*, or marriage chest, made in the Italian Renaissance style. To the right of the bed is an Italian chest of drawers made of rosewood, burr maple or birch, and mahogany with intricate gilt wood inlay. A notable decorative object is the Persian-influenced vase of ceramic, enamel, and metal, which was converted into an electric lamp in the first half of the 20th century.

LEFT: *This engraving by the German printmaker Friedrick Muller is after the painting* La Madonna di San Sisto *(the Sistine Madonna), by Renaissance artist Raphael Sanzio. One of his most recognizable works,* La Madonna di San Sisto *features Raphael's famous portrayal of little angels at the bottom of the painting.*

SHERATON ROOM This elegant, sophisticated room is named for one of the foremost English furniture designers, Thomas Sheraton (1751–1806). His furniture designs, published in three widely read pattern books, were influential in the development of neoclassical decorating styles at the turn of the 19th century.

It would have been popular at the time to use classical wall coverings and fabrics in muted tones, as seen here in the wallpaper, bed hangings, and window draperies.

The English satinwood and mahogany furniture pieces in the Sheraton style—including a double desk, square-back sofa, and night-stand—are typically light and delicate, with tapered legs and graceful silhouettes.

Over the fireplace is a portrait of George Vanderbilt with siblings Frederick and Lila as children; George, the dark-haired boy on the left, would have been five years old when he sat for the artist Jacob H. Lazarus (1822–91) in 1867. On the other side of the doorway is a Currier & Ives print depicting William Henry Vanderbilt racing his famous trotters, Aldine and Maud S. (the latter bought for $20,000 in 1878).

FAR RIGHT: *The satinwood tester bed in the Sheraton Room is elegantly draped with peach silk hangings and painted with bows, cherubs, and garlands. The piece is based on a plate (right) in Thomas Sheraton's first pattern book,* The Cabinet-Maker and Upholsterer's Drawing Book, *published between 1791 and 1794. The Biltmore House Library contains an original copy of this volume.*

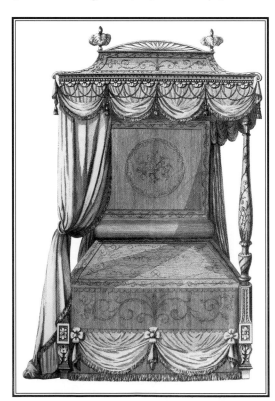

ABOVE: *The leaded-glass firescreen in the Chippendale Room was given to Hunt by the construction crew that worked on Biltmore House and purchased by Mr. William A.V. Cecil for the Biltmore House collection in 1985.*

RIGHT: *The Young Algerian Girl is one of two paintings in the room by Pierre-Auguste Renoir (1841–1919), a leading French Impressionist whose work first became popular in America at the turn of the century.*

CHIPPENDALE ROOM Like the Sheraton Room, this guest room reflects the popularity of an important English furniture maker. Thomas Chippendale (1718–79) was the first to bring out a pattern book devoted entirely to furniture. In *The Gentleman and Cabinet-Maker's Director*, published in 1754, he presented a range of elaborate designs adapted from the Louis XV style and thereby influenced the fashion for fancy interiors.

Exemplifying the Chippendale style are the tester bed and seating furniture, which were made in 18th- and 19th-century England. These mahogany pieces include such typical stylistic elements as curved cabriole legs, hairy-paw feet, and carved leaf and shell motifs. Also in keeping with the period is the use of coordinating wallpaper and fabrics.

OLD ENGLISH ROOM Decorated in the Jacobean style, this room provides an appropriate setting for the upholstered furniture, reproductions of 17th-century originals at Knole in Kent, England. The designs feature mechanical parts adjusted by ratchets, allowing the sofa, for example, to be converted into a daybed.

On display are several Cecil family portraits, which came into the collection after Cornelia Vanderbilt married the Honorable John Francis Amherst Cecil in 1924. Over the mantel is the Great Lord Burghley, William Cecil; above the oak chest are his grandchildren William and Frances, painted in 1599 by the Italian artist Frederico Zuccaro (1543–1609). Between the two 16th-century portraits is their descendant, John Cecil.

ABOVE LEFT: *Among the family likenesses in the 17th-century-style Old English Room are William and Frances Cecil (left) and Lord Burghley (above right), who was a principal minister to Queen Elizabeth I between 1558 and his death in 1598. The latter portrait was finished in 1589 by the Flemish painter Marcus Gheeraerts the Younger (1561–1636), a favorite artist of English royalty.*

*T*HE DOWNSTAIRS LEVEL OF BILTMORE HOUSE SERVED three distinct purposes. It contained the recreation areas that were used by the Vanderbilts and their guests. It also housed the bedrooms and common rooms for the "below stairs" staff. And, as was customary in great country estates, the basement accommodated the pantries and service areas, designed to keep kitchen and laundry clamor far removed from the living quarters upstairs.

HALLOWEEN ROOM This one-time storage area was taken over in 1924 by Cornelia and John Cecil and their guests for a party during their wedding festivities. Guests personally painted different sections on the walls, thus creating the unusual decoration.

BOWLING ALLEY The sport of bowling arrived in America in the 1600s with the Dutch settlers and had become a popular pastime by the 1800s, as Victorian men patronized an ever-increasing number of public lanes. At Biltmore both men and women played on one of the first bowling alleys in a private home. The lanes were installed in 1895 by the Brunswick-Balke-Collender Company, a top manufacturer of recreation equipment, and were constructed just as alleys are today. Durable maple planks were laid along the first third of the lanes, which takes the most wear from balls striking the surface, and softer pine decking was used on the remainder, where the balls roll. Balls were returned and pins reset by hand.

DRESSING ROOMS In the 1890s, each activity had its own dress code, for which ladies and gentlemen had to change their clothes several times a day. To change for recreation, guests used the Dressing Rooms, which were arrayed along separate halls for men and women. These private chambers guaranteed that no one would have to make a long, potentially embarrassing trip from bedroom to basement immodestly attired.

OPPOSITE: *Wooden balls of different sizes indicate that a variety of games besides tenpins could be played in the Bowling Alley.* LEFT: *In the main Dressing Room, Cornelia Vanderbilt's ivory grooming set is displayed on a 19th-century English mahogany dressing table; a wooden towel rack holds fresh linens.* ABOVE: *This figure is part of the imaginative mural painted for a party in the Halloween Room in 1924.*

SWIMMING POOL Biltmore offered a wide range of recreational activities—reflecting not only the need for entertainment in a remote mountain region but also the new emphasis placed on health, fitness, and exercise in the late 1800s. Among the most popular diversions was bathing, which lured Victorians to seashore and lakeside resorts each summer.

The Vanderbilts and their guests, however, could enjoy the water in any season—in a 70,000-gallon indoor pool. Measuring 53 feet long by 27 feet wide by 8½ feet deep, the tile-work pool was equipped with such amenities as underwater lighting, safety ropes, and a diving platform. It was fed with hot water through the black hose; the large standing pipe supplied cold water.

Illuminated by chandeliers, the room is also one of the best places to see the fireproof, terra-cotta tile vaulting that appears in several areas of the House. The vaults were installed according to a technologically advanced building system developed by Rafael Guastavino; his technique was favored by architects because it allowed masonry vaulting to cover wide spans without interior supports during construction.

GYMNASIUM The Gymnasium was primarily a male precinct. Here, family and guests could tone their muscles with the most up-to-date apparatus, including parallel bars, a chain-driven rowing machine, and wall-mounted pulleys with adjustable weights. The gym also offered barbells, medicine balls, Indian clubs (used to improve hand-eye coordination), and, for the refined athlete, a fencing set. After a vigorous workout, guests could cool down in the showers.

LEFT: *Both men and women would have worn bathing costumes that reached down to the knee and up to the neck when enjoying the indoor pool.* INSET, OPPOSITE: *Much of the 19th-century equipment in the Gymnasium, including the exercise machines, parallel bars, and Indian clubs, was manufactured by A. G. Spalding & Bro., which is still a prominent sporting-goods company today.*

PANTRIES Accommodating the large number of family members, guests, and staff at Biltmore required an extensive larder—especially when provisions were bought in bulk. One bill of sale from 1896, for example, records an order for 28 pounds of lamb legs and loins, 52 pounds of prime beef ribs, 22 broiling and roasting chickens, 62 pounds of muskmelons, and two baskets of peaches.

Groceries from shops in Asheville's Central Market, as well as fresh produce, meats, and dairy products from Biltmore's farm operation, were kept in a series of pantries. The Vegetable Pantry held bins of fruits and vegetables; the Small Pantry stored canned goods; the Housekeeper's Pantry also had canned goods, along with a desk used by the head housekeeper; and the Canning Pantry would

have contained produce put up on the Estate.

WALK-IN REFRIGERATORS Perishables were preserved in two spacious walk-in food lockers that were cooled by a chilled brine solution circulating through pipes in their interiors. Any sort of refrigeration, let alone cold storage on this scale, was a novelty in the late 1800s, when most homes still relied on iceboxes and springhouses.

SERVANTS' BEDROOMS At any one time 40-50 servants might be employed at Biltmore, where they lived near their work stations in separate halls according to sex and rank. The bedrooms along this corridor represent the private quarters for female members of the kitchen staff, which included cooks' assistants and scullery maids. The rooms are airy and comfortable, with splint-seat chairs, chestnut dressers and ward-

robes, and iron beds and washstands holding monogrammed chamber sets.

Based upon their duties and the time of day, service dress changed accordingly. For instance, maids wore pink uniforms with white collars and cuffs in the morning and black with white trim in the evening; a cook's assistant wore a red-checked pinafore and a dust cap.

Mounted on the wall outside the bedrooms is one of several call boxes found throughout the House. It is part of an ingenious electric communication system that enabled servants to be summoned with a mere touch of a button from most of the upstairs rooms. The boxes registered a call by ringing a bell and raising a little arrow that indicated the room from which it originated.

OPPOSITE TOP: *The spacious Housekeeper's Pantry doubled as a storage area and an office for the head housekeeper, whose job entailed inventorying and replenishing supplies.*
OPPOSITE BOTTOM: *Walk-in food lockers stored the quantities of food required for Biltmore's large household.*

ABOVE: *One of more than 60 staff rooms, this simply furnished Servant's Bedroom includes a cast-iron bed and washstand. Such inexpensive pieces were first made in the mid-1800s and soon became popular among health-conscious Victorians, who believed that metal, unlike wood, did not harbor germs.*

PASTRY KITCHEN Biltmore's kitchen complex, comparable in size to that of a large hotel, was designed for maximum efficiency in food preparation and service. Cooking chores were carried out in three specialized areas, each finished with tiled floors and walls for easy maintenance and each fully stocked with the latest culinary equipment. Staffed by a large number of chefs, cooks, and maids, the kitchens turned out everything from a cup of tea to the lavish banquets that were in vogue at the turn of the century; indeed, a formal dinner could include up to 20 courses and last for several hours.

The Pastry Kitchen was used for fine baking and provided all manner of popular breads and rich confections (a 19th-century cookbook might list hundreds of recipes for cakes and pies). Dough was rolled out on the marble-topped table built in beneath the window; stone slabs like this are preferred by bakers because dough is less likely to stick to the surface. Pastries were baked in two ovens, and dough and perishable ingredients were kept chilled in a refrigerator.

ROTISSERIE KITCHEN Another cooking area is the Rotisserie Kitchen, which was used for roasting meat, poultry, and game. Such foods—especially pheasant, duck, venison, and other animals brought back from shooting parties—figured heavily on 19th-century menus, often being served for several courses in the same meal.

The iron rotisserie oven, fueled by wood or coal, features a mechanized rotary spit whose speed can be regulated by the electric rheostat mounted on the wall. A drip pan caught grease spatters, and a large overhead vent hood drew off smoke.

OPPOSITE: *While bread was sometimes ordered from the French Bakery in Asheville, most baked goods served on Biltmore's tables were made in the Pastry Kitchen.* ABOVE: *Meats were roasted over an open fire in the rotisserie oven.* LEFT: The Encyclopædia of Practical Cookery, *from Biltmore's book collection, was published in London around 1893; it offers instruction on trussing meat and suggestions for "artistic" supper dishes.*

ABOVE: *The Main Kitchen is well stocked with such tools of the chef's trade as copper cookware, knives, sharpening steels, and choppers. The metal serving trolley, fitted with chafing dishes, was used to transport hot foods to the upstairs dining rooms.*

OPPOSITE TOP: *The electric dumbwaiter in the Kitchen Pantry has push-button controls and runs 38 feet between the basement and second floor.*

OPPOSITE BOTTOM: *This hand-cranked, tin "chopping machine" was the 19th-century equivalent of a food processor.*

MAIN KITCHEN Most of the cooking at Biltmore took place in the roomy Main Kitchen. Work here started early each morning, when the scullery maid stoked the firebox of the cast-iron cookstove with wood or coal; then the kitchen staff set the work table with knives, choppers, cleavers, braising mallets, and other utensils for the chefs. Conveniently overhead is a battery of polished copper pots and pans—considered the

premier cookware for its ability to conduct and retain heat evenly. Displayed around the room are such accessories as a coffee mill and sausage stuffer; in the corner is a large mortar and pestle.

On one side of the stove, which is seven and a half feet long, is a small, separate grill and on the other is a tall iron cabinet. Custom made by the New York firm of Duparquet, Huot & Moneuse, it held pots, pans and serving dishes. Of particular note are the cabinet's counter-balanced sliding doors, which, unlike standard hinged doors, allowed access without interfering with the kitchen's work space.

KITCHEN PANTRY Meals prepared in the basement kitchens had to be transported to the first-floor Butler's Pantry, outside the Banquet Hall, where they were transferred onto serving dishes. (The servants responsible for this chore were familiarly called "tweenies," as they brought food between the kitchens and dining rooms.) While a warming cart was often used for carrying food, meals could also be sent upstairs from the Kitchen Pantry via two dumbwaiters—one manual, one electric; the latter had a lifting capacity of 250 pounds and an operating speed of 100 feet per minute. This room was also used for storing china and washing dishes.

SERVANTS' DINING ROOM The domestic staff at Biltmore was ordered in a strict hierarchy, as was traditional in the late 1800s. The chef, butler, housekeeper, valet, and lady's maid were among the upper servants, while the footman, chamber maids, houseboy, and scullery maid were considered the lower servants. The groups rarely ate or socialized together. In the Servants' Dining Room, which was one of several areas used for staff meals, the servants ate in shifts, with the senior staff taking their place at the table first—cooked for and waited on by the lower-ranking staff.

SERVANTS' SITTING ROOM Like the upstairs Living Halls used by family and guests, this room functioned as a gathering place for servants passing the time or awaiting a call to work. Here they might have read, written letters, played cards, or listened to the Victrola.

ORGAN MOTOR ROOM This room was designed to house the blower mechanism for the Banquet Hall organ and contains the air chase and electrical wiring necessary to power the 19th-century Skinner instrument. Because an organ was not installed when the House was built, the room was used for storage until 1998, when an organ was finally installed.

WORK ROOM This room is used by the floral design staff to prepare the cut-flower arrangements seen throughout the House. Plants from the gardens and greenhouses have always played an important role in the decor at Biltmore.

OPPOSITE: *Staff ate in the Servants' Dining Room around a mahogany dining table, seated on bentwood chairs.* ABOVE: *Servants used this sitting room in their free time to write letters on an oak desk, made by Biltmore Estate Industries, or play records on the early-20th-century RCA Victrola.* RIGHT: *This Autoharp, a zither-like instrument used to accompany singing, was made by the Zimmerman Autoharp Company, Dolgeville, New York.*

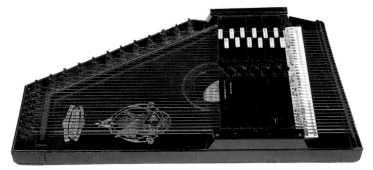

BROWN LAUNDRY Like the kitchens, Biltmore's laundry complex was a convenient, efficient operation organized on a commercial scale. In four specialized work rooms, the laundress and maids handled the substantial quantities of clothing and linens generated by family, guests, and servants.

The Brown Laundry was used for staff laundry and hand washables and is equipped with deep tubs in which dirt was laboriously scrubbed away on fluted-tin washboards. The wooden "cradle" is a hand-agitated mechanical washing machine from the early 1900s. On the table are various pressing devices, including fluting irons with ridged rollers for crimping pleats and ruffles and double-pointed sadirons that were heated on a special laundry stove. Next door is the Laundresses' Toilet, which was for staff use.

MAIN LAUNDRY The equipment in the Main Laundry is similar to the state-of-the-art machinery originally installed in 1895. In addition to a belt-driven barrel washer are an extractor, which was used to spin out excess water, and a mangle, which was used for pressing.

DRYING ROOM On the right side of the Main Laundry is the Drying Room; all laundry was dried indoors, so that the laundress would never be at the mercy of the weather. After the laundry was wrung as dry as possible, it was draped over an innovative system of rolling wooden racks that could be pulled out from a wall cabinet for air drying or pushed back into niches that were heated with electric coils running along the floor.

OPPOSITE: *Linens aired on pull-out racks, which slid into recesses in a wall cabinet where heat from floor-mounted electric coils speeded drying.* INSET, LEFT: *This sadiron, made by the Enterprise Manufacturing Company of Philadelphia, features a detachable stay-cool wooden handle that could be used interchangeably on iron bodies heating on a laundry stove.* BELOW: *In the Brown Laundry, hand washing was done with wooden washboards in the enameled basins.*

*S*ET OFF FROM THE REST OF THE FIRST FLOOR IS the Bachelors' Wing, a private, masculine section of the House with its own entrance through a covered carriage porch off the stable courtyard. It was connected to the single men's upstairs guest rooms by a separate stairwell and boasted specialized game and sitting areas where gentlemen could discuss business and politics, relax with a pipe, or relive exploits from a day's shooting party.

OPPOSITE: *With its ebonized woodwork and gold-leaf wall covering, the Gun Room is a handsome showcase for hunting trophies, such as this game bird (above), and sporting art. The room also displayed guns; collecting antique and contemporary firearms was a popular gentlemen's pastime.* RIGHT: *In turn-of-the-century society, smoking was an acceptable practice—for men at least—as long as it was done in a separate room. The Smoking Room provided a comfortable retreat for male guests to enjoy after-dinner cigars.*

SMOKING ROOM Smoking, like gambling and hunting, was primarily a male prerogative in the 1800s, and the smoking parlor became a required feature in fashionable country houses soon after it appeared in mid-century. Here, men savored the pleasure of a cigar or pipe, perhaps as an accompaniment to a glass of after-dinner spirits; they might even try the new machine-rolled cigarettes being produced in the tobacco centers of North Carolina. Guests could also select a leather-bound book from the collection and read before the fire in the plush 17th-century-style sofas and chairs.

GUN ROOM Guests at Biltmore never wanted for outdoor recreation. There was horseback riding, carriage driving, fishing, hiking, and, of course, hunting—the quintessential country house amusement. To ensure a good day's shooting, Mr. Vanderbilt had the Estate stocked with a plentiful supply of deer, quail, pheasant, and other wild game.

The Gun Room pays tribute to the popularity of the sport, which had developed into such a passion by the 1870s that the proper house was considered incomplete without this special shrine. As was customary, the room is outfitted with glass-front cases for firearms (now in storage), stored in custom-built racks, and for an array of animal trophies. On the walls are 19th-century prints with sporting themes after the British artists Sir Joshua Reynolds (1723–92) and James Ward (1769–1859), and on the tables are bronze sculptures of game animals and a hunting dog.

*I*N THE PREAUTOMOTIVE AGE OF THE LATE 19TH century, horses and horse-drawn vehicles played an important role in both transportation and recreation. Reflecting their significance is the 12,000-square-foot stable complex at the north end of the front facade — a facility that was as carefully designed and completely equipped as the House itself.

STABLE Like his father, who was so devoted to his trotters that he built an indoor riding ring for them, Mr. Vanderbilt took exceptional care of his horses. As many as 25 riding and driving horses, along with 20 carriages, were sheltered at Biltmore in a modern stable complete with electricity, plumbing, glazed-brick walls, and brass fixtures and hardware.

The Stable also contained all the attendant service areas, including rooms for saddles, tack, harness, blankets, and feed, as well as the Estate offices and living quarters for single male servants. Among the staff of stable hands were grooms, a harness man, an exerciser, and a coachman, whose job entailed supervising the grooming of the horses, driving family and guests in the carriages, and assisting riders with their mounts.

Today, the Stable has been converted into an avenue of shops offering books, confections, toys, Christmas ornaments, and decorative accessories. The largest shop is located in the former Carriage House, while a café now occupies the old horse stable — with tables tucked into the original box stalls. In the courtyard, where horses' hooves and carriage wheels once clattered on the brick pavers, tables and chairs are set out for dining or relaxing in the historic setting.

ABOVE: *The Stable was still under construction in the spring of 1894. On Olmsted's advice, it was located at the north end of the House to buffer the gardens from wind.* RIGHT: *Riders posed on their mounts on the Front Lawn around 1900.* OPPOSITE: *Horses and carriages would arrive in the Stable courtyard through the arched Porte Cochere. On the center dormer is a "master" clock, which electrically controls the clocks in the servants' quarters.*

Biltmore Gardens and Trails

From mountain forest to mani-
cured flower bed to valley farm, the grounds
at Biltmore were unparalleled in scale and
diversity when conceived in the 1880s. They
remain one of the premier achievements of
America's foremost landscape architect, Frederick Law Olmsted. His genius for design and
his love of nature are visible today throughout
the 8,000-acre Estate, where his plan and many
of the original plantings have been preserved.

*W*HAT IS NOW A LUSH, MATURE LANDSCAPE WAS once a depleted tract of worn-out farms and cutover woodlands. Olmsted transformed the site into a 250-acre park, designed in the English pastoral mode to complement the architecture of the House, take advantage of the native flora and terrain, and provide varied settings for outdoor recreation. Beginning with the formal lawns around the House, the grounds become increasingly naturalistic as they spread out toward a managed woodland that looks so wild it appears never to have been touched. The Estate includes miles of scenic carriage drives, several lakes and ponds, and thousands of acres of managed forests.

APPROACH ROAD An integral part of Biltmore's landscape is the three-mile-long Approach Road. It begins at the Lodge Gate, the pebbledash gatehouse at the edge of Biltmore Village, and ends at the sphinx-topped stone pillars near the Front Lawn. In between it traverses a "garden" as meticulously planned as the formal flower beds.

Olmsted designed the Approach Road to heighten anticipation of seeing the House by having visitors first wind slowly through a woodland. The idea, he said, was to evoke a sense of mystery while creating the "…sensation of passing through the remote depths of a natural forest." And so the drive snakes along the ravines through dense border plantings of rhododendron, mountain laurel, and azalea, passing from woods to open meadow and back again to groves of hemlock and pine—with no distant views to interrupt the intimate effect. At every turn is a new surprise: a stream, a pool, a blanket of wildflowers, a thicket of river cane.

In developing this "natural" landscape, Olmsted started virtually from scratch, sculpting the land before installing any plant material. Many of the trees and shrubs he used were transplants collected as seedlings from the Carolina plains, piedmont, and mountains. These native specimens were supplemented with plants grown in Biltmore's own nursery, which had been established in 1889 with stock and seeds from the acclaimed Arnold Arboretum near Boston, as well as from other nurseries in America and Europe.

Because the family traveled frequently— "Mr. Vanderbilt and his guests always miss the best of the bloom," lamented Olmsted—the Approach Road was planted with a variety of deciduous trees, conifers, and flowering shrubs that would provide interest year-round. There were even exotic species, such as bamboo, to add a subtropical character to the landscape. The design was acknowledged to be a success, even by so particular a critic as Richard Morris Hunt. "Hasn't Olmsted done wonders with the approach road?" he wrote in an 1892 letter to Mr. Vanderbilt. "It alone will give him lasting fame."

OPPOSITE: Designed by Hunt, the Lodge Gate was built with bricks and roof tiles made on the Estate; it is faced with a rough stucco finish called pebbledash. BOTTOM: Mr. Vanderbilt, standing beside Olmsted (far right, front row), poses with the crew during construction of the Approach Road in 1892. BELOW: The drive is lined with dense border plantings to create a mysterious, intimate effect.

ESPLANADE At the end of the Approach Road, Biltmore House at last comes into view, rising before a trim, level lawn lined with double rows of tulip trees. The contrast in style between the naturalistic drive and the formal grounds immediately surrounding the House is deliberate: Olmsted used this area to form a transition between the stately building and the wilder, outlying landscape.

The entire forecourt is called the Esplanade and was inspired by the gardens at the mid-17th-century Château de Vaux-le-Vicomte near Melun, France. It incorporates the Front Lawn, with its softly splashing fountain, and the majestic Rampe Douce (meaning "gentle incline"), a graduated stairway zigzagging along a rough-cut limestone wall. Beyond stretches a grassy slope known as the Vista, with a statue of Diana, goddess of the hunt, marking the summit—the perfect vantage point for viewing the House against its backdrop of mountains.

TERRACES Visitors at Biltmore, who would often stay for weeks or months at a time, were encouraged to use the entire landscape—whether by hiking through the forest, playing lawn games, or simply watching the sunset from the comfort of a garden bench. The Terraces were designed for those who preferred to stay close by the House. Guests could enjoy the shade of the Library Terrace, which is sheltered by an arbor of fragrant wisteria and colorful trumpet creeper. Or they might stroll to the South Terrace, once the site of a bowling green, to relax in the limestone teahouse and take in the spectacular panorama of the deerpark, Lagoon, and Blue Ridge Mountains; Mount Pisgah, at 5,897 feet, is the highest peak in the distance.

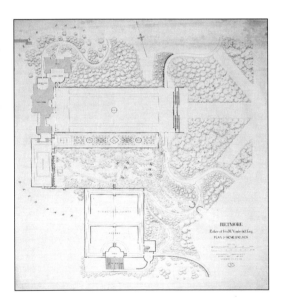

ABOVE LEFT: *Olmsted's original plan for the Home Grounds covered the design for garden areas around the House—from the Esplanade to the Walled Garden.*

ABOVE RIGHT: *The Rampe Douce was already completed by December 1892, while the rest of the Esplanade and the House were still under construction.*

INSET, ABOVE: *Young Cornelia takes a dip in the Front Lawn fountain in this circa 1910 photo.* OPPOSITE: *The statue of Diana stands before a double grove of hemlock trees that seem to form the letter "V"; the Rampe Douce is at the base of the slope. The lawn between was originally mowed by a horse- or mule-drawn mowing machine.*

BELOW: *Water lilies and Egyptian lotus fill the pools in the Italian Garden; in warm weather the bed in the central pool is stocked with cannas and ornamental grasses, both popular in turn-of-the-century gardens.* **OPPOSITE:** *A path threads past forsythia, pink and white dogwood, holly, and white-flowering crab apple in the Ramble. The garden is so lush and varied that the promenade seems longer than it actually is.*

ITALIAN GARDEN Three symmetrical pools mark the Italian Garden, where gravel paths and manicured lawns form an ordered composition. Enclosed by a hemlock hedge and stone walls, the garden was intended as a separate outdoor "room" and is decorated with classical statuary, jardinieres, and benches. While the space was meant for quiet contemplation, it was also used for recreation: tennis and croquet were played on the grassy area nearest the House. After their game, guests could slip into the basement to change clothes through the door under the stairway.

PERGOLA Another broad stone stair leads to the wisteria- and trumpet-creeper-covered Pergola overlooking the former lawn tennis court. The shady bower provided a cool spot for spectators, who could also enjoy the soft music of trickling wall fountains.

SHRUB GARDEN In contrast to the formal Italian Garden is the four-acre Shrub Garden, or Ramble—a rich, picturesque landscape with hundreds of woody plants. Olmsted chose this protected site for a "secluded and genial" garden where guests could "ramble" along meandering paths through an ever-changing pageant of plants. Filled with specimens that provide a succession of color—from the winter jasmine that opens in February to the cut-leaf Japanese maples that blush red until frost—this area features such old-fashioned shrubs as lilac, viburnum, forsythia, and honeysuckle. It also includes numerous species native to Asia, such as Japanese stewartia, kousa dogwood, and, added after the turn of the century, Yoshino cherry, reflecting the era's interest in plants from the Far East.

WALLED GARDEN The gate at the lower edge of the Ramble opens into the four-acre Walled Garden, which Olmsted had planned with mixed plots of flowers, fruits, and vegetables typical of an English kitchen garden. Mr. Vanderbilt, however, insisted on a "garden of ornament rather than utility," reasoning that the Estate farm would supply produce instead.

Two arbors totalling 236 feet entwined with many original vines form the spine of the symmetrical plan, which comprises flower beds arranged in patterns similar to an Elizabethan knot garden. The garden blooms with a progression of color, starting in spring with daffodils, hyacinths, and tulips. These are followed in summer by some 40 varieties of annuals, including dahlias, zinnias, and globe amaranth, while fall brings a multi-hued display of chrysanthemums. Along the outer walls are espaliered fruit trees, rose-of-Sharon, and pyracantha—which require trimming at least six times per growing season—as well as perennial borders of bleeding heart, peony, iris, and daylily.

ROSE GARDEN The lower half of the walled area is planted with about 2,300 roses in more than 250 varieties, including 159 All-America Rose Selections. While most of the plants are modern varieties, the garden also boasts a number of heirloom roses—especially varieties grown for the Vanderbilts, such as Paul Neyron (introduced in 1869) and American Beauty (introduced in 1875).

CONSERVATORY The glass-roofed conservatory was designed by Hunt, rebuilt in 1957, and restored in 1999. It provides flowers and plants for Biltmore House and tender bedding plants for the gardens—just as it did in the Vanderbilts' day. The building—sheltered in a valley for protection—was constructed at the lower end of the garden so as to not obstruct views from the House. Its central room is a "Palm House," where a large collection of palms, ferns, and other foliage plants thrive. Annexes include a cool house, hot house, and orchid house. The lower level has been converted into *A Gardener's Place* shop, offering plants and garden accessories.

OPPOSITE: *The Walled Garden is abloom with thousands of daffodils and Dutch tulips in spring. Such enclosed gardens were common in England and northern Europe because they trapped sunshine and shielded plants from wind, creating a hospitable microclimate.*

INSET, LEFT: *Among the 250 varieties in the Rose Garden is the Pink Peace rose, a fragrant, long-blooming hybrid tea introduced in 1959.*

BELOW: *The beds in front of the Conservatory are filled with buddleia, asters, sunflowers, and other colorful plants that attract butterflies.*

SPRING GARDEN Sheltered by a cathedral grove of white pines and hemlocks, the Spring Garden lies in a secluded pocket just beyond the Ramble. The garden was named for the two small springs found here, which Olmsted diverted underground to create a stream flowing into the Azalea Garden. He also called it the Vernal Garden for its spring-blooming shrubs, such as forsythia, spirea, deutzia, and mock orange.

AZALEA GARDEN A wood-chip path connects the Spring Garden to the 20-acre Azalea Garden, the largest and "lowest" of the gardens that occupy a series of hollows below the House. Olmsted called it the Glen, for its protected valley site. Today, however, it is named—and renowned—for its superb array of azaleas.

These plants were assembled by Chauncey Beadle, a Cornell-educated horticulturist who was hired "temporarily" in 1890 to oversee the nursery but stayed on until his death in 1950, eventually becoming estate superintendent. Over the course of 15 years, Beadle and three friends, who called themselves the "Azalea Hunters," traveled from New England to Florida to Texas studying and gathering native specimens. In 1940, he donated his entire collection of 3,000 plants—one of the largest collections in the world—to Biltmore Estate.

More than 1,000 azaleas, representing 14 native species and countless hybrids, now thrive in the garden, growing alongside metasequoias, magnolias, dogwoods, and a number of conifers that Beadle added from an arboretum that was never completed. Included in the vast variety of plants are such rarities as the Florida torreya, now facing extinction in its natural habitat, and the Franklinia, which disappeared from the wild in 1790.

OPPOSITE: The naturalistic Azalea Garden was originally planted with a variety of shrubs, flowers, and ground covers. It now features one of the most complete collections of native azaleas in existence, along with numerous hybrids, such as these Asiatic specimens surrounded by stewartia, hemlock, spruce, and dogwood. LEFT: Edged with towering pines and hemlocks, the Spring Garden teems with early-blooming forsythia and redbuds surrounding a grassy glade. INSET, LEFT: Chauncey Beadle, shown in 1949 among his beloved azaleas, was hired in 1890 because Olmsted was impressed with the young horticulturist's "encyclopedic knowledge of plants." He said that he came to Biltmore for a month and stayed a lifetime.

DEER PARK Covering 250 acres to the south and west of Biltmore House is a wooded area known as a deer park, inspiring the name of an Estate restaurant. Scenic game preserves like this were often used for hunting on English country estates. The natural design, composed of rolling meadows and groves of poplar, beech, oak, and hickory, was inspired by the "pastoral" landscape style developed in the 1700s.

BASS POND AND LAGOON Water features were an important aspect of the pastoral land-scape, and Olmsted planned two for the Estate. The Bass Pond, created from an old creek-fed millpond, is just south of the Azalea Garden. Guests out for a walk at the "end" of the gardens could rest at the boathouse or take in the view from a footbridge spanning a waterfall that spills into a rocky ravine. In addition to its beauty, the Pond is remarkable for an engineering feat: Olmsted installed a flume system for flood control that pipes debris-filled storm water under the lake bed.

The placid Lagoon is located on the lower drive and acts as a mirror for the maple, sweet gum, and river birch lining its shore and for the western facade of the House. Like the Bass Pond, the Lagoon was used for recreation.

LEFT: *The tranquil Lagoon was used by guests for fishing and rowing.* ABOVE: *The rustic boathouse overlooking the Bass Pond offers a peaceful resting place after a garden stroll; Olmsted incorporated similar structures into his designs for many public parks.* INSET, BELOW: *In autumn the hardwoods in the deer park put on a splendid foliage display. Olmsted created such serene pastoral settings to have a soothing effect on the spirit.*

WALKING TRAILS Near the Bass Pond and Azalea Garden are four walking trails carrying out Frederick Law Olmsted's philosophy that Biltmore's landscape should be enjoyed to its fullest. The trails are based on Olmsted's early plans for the Bass Pond, providing vantage points to observe birds and animals that live on the Estate.

The Bass Pond Trail offers a spectacular view of the brick bridge across the pond. The Meadow Trail loops through the deer park, with views of the pond and wildflower meadows.

Passing through a shady grove, the Creekside Trail showcases a bald cypress more than 100 feet high growing on the opposite bank. Part of the Woodland Trail follows an old farm road dating to the 1880s; today, the area is evidence of the Estate's reforestation efforts. A rustic bridge of native black locust, pine, and cedar some 50 feet long spans a spring-fed brook in the wooded hollow.

FOREST While the rich woodlands blanketing much of the Estate seem to be virgin stands, many were planted as part of a comprehensive land management program initiated by Olmsted and developed by Gifford Pinchot, the first American-born trained forester to practice in the United States.

Biltmore's woods had been badly overfarmed, overcut, and burned before Mr. Vanderbilt acquired the property—so much that Olmsted advised him against installing an extensive European-style park. The designer proposed turning the site into productive timberland that would contribute to the Estate and also represent America's first organized attempt at forestry. In 1891, Olmsted enlisted Pinchot to rehabilitate the woodland. Pinchot's plan—identifying varieties, selectively thinning, and planting for maximum timber yield—served as a national model.

Pinchot left Biltmore in 1895 to establish what would become the U.S. Forest Service; continuing his work was Dr. Carl Schenck (1868–1955), a prominent German forester Mr. Vanderbilt invited to America. Besides installing experimental plantations of indigenous species, Schenck founded the Biltmore Forest School in 1898. The school operated until 1913, teaching conservation techniques still influential today.

There are now about 4,500 acres of forest at Biltmore, with timber sales providing some financial support for Estate operations. The land is actively managed to improve the quality of soil, water, and wildlife habitats, and to preserve the forest in harmony with Olmsted's historic landscape.

OPPOSITE: *The shade-dappled Woodland Trail crosses a 50-foot bridge crafted of cedar rails and posts, locust pickets, and pine beams and planking.*
LEFT: *Forester Gifford Pinchot (left) was photographed on the Estate with Mr. Vanderbilt (second from right) and guests around 1895; Pinchot went on to found the Yale University School of Forestry and the U.S. Forest Service.*

Biltmore Estate Winery

O PENED IN 1985, BILTMORE ESTATE

Winery is a fitting addition to Mr. Vanderbilt's

vision. The enterprise not only recalls the

historic estate wineries of Europe but also

reaffirms the century-old Biltmore tradition of

self-sufficiency. Although one of the "youngest"

wineries in America, it has become the most

visited and among the most acclaimed, having

earned more than 100 awards in its first decade.

*J*UST AS BILTMORE HOUSE PRESERVES THE ARCHI-
tectural heritage of the Estate, the Winery perpetuates its agricultural legacy. Rich farmland that once supported produce crops has
been given over to vineyards, and the former dairy complex now
houses the extensive wine-making operation. The Winery also carries on Mr. Vanderbilt's interest in technology and insistence on quality: state-of-the-art
equipment is used at every step in producing Biltmore's premier wines.

WINERY The Winery is located in a building
designed by Richard Morris Hunt for Biltmore's
dairy, which began in 1896 as part of a large
farm operation that also included produce and
livestock. Like Biltmore House, the dairy barn
was thoroughly modern—from the ice-cooled
pipeline that delivered milk into a creamery that
once stood across the street to the underground
rail system that hauled away used stall bedding.
The dairy became one of the Estate's most successful enterprises: its eggs, milk, butter, and
cheese were sold throughout Asheville and the
Southeast, and ice cream was served at a dairy
bar next to this main building.

The facility was occupied by the dairy until 1958 and was reopened as
the Winery in 1985 after a
three-year renovation. Covering 96,500 square feet, the
handsome pebbledash building
proved remarkably adaptable in
being converted to a new use.
The old haymow became visitors' areas, and the
three wings of the barn, where more than 200
cows had been housed, were turned into tasting
and bottling rooms. The structural vaults in the
basement, which have a constant temperature of
54 degrees—the perfect temperature for a wine
cellar—were an ideal place to keep wines and
sparkling wines during aging.

OPPOSITE: *After a three-year
renovation, the former dairy
became the Winery. Its central
clock tower originally had only
three working clock faces; the
side toward the pasture
featured a painted-on clock,
as the grazing cows did not
need to know the time.*
ABOVE: *Biltmore Dairy Farms
milkmen, seen here around
1930, delivered milk, cheese,
butter, and eggs in their fleet
of dry-ice-cooled trucks.* LEFT:
*An aerial photograph from the
1920s shows the unusual
design of the dairy barn, with
its three long wings. Today
these have been converted to
house the Winery's Tasting
and Bottling Rooms.*

VINEYARDS Biltmore began experimenting with wine making in the 1970s. The first vines were planted in 1971, in a plot near the Conservatory greenhouses, and the first wines produced six years later (it generally takes five years for vines to mature enough to yield a full crop). The regional climate—with its warm days, cool nights, and mild winter temperatures—is quite hospitable to grapes; in fact, wine has been made in North Carolina as far back as the colonial era.

While the vineyards were initially planted with indigenous grapes, then with French-American hybrids, they have now been given over to *Vitis vinifera*—the European grape species from which all world-class wines are produced. Some 48,000 vines thrive on more than 70 gently sloping acres in the western portion of the Estate, constituting one of the largest plantings of vinifera grapes east of the Mississippi River. A lake was constructed on the site to insure a favorable microclimate: the water creates a little pocket of warmth beside the vineyards, helping combat the late spring frosts that threaten young buds.

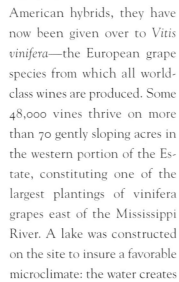

Among the grape varieties under cultivation are Cabernet Sauvignon, Cabernet Franc, and Merlot, which yield red wines, along with Chardonnay and Riesling, which are used in making white wines. Chardonnay grapes also go into the sparkling wine.

Each year between late August and mid-October, Biltmore's employees gather in the vineyards to pick grapes under the supervision of Bernard Delille, a classically trained wine master from France. The clusters are painstakingly picked by hand to ensure that only ripe, perfect "berries" are selected. With a harvest exceeding 200 tons of grapes annually, the vineyards satisfy a fourth of the Winery's production capacity.

ABOVE: *At harvest time clusters of grapes are picked by hand under the direction of Biltmore's French wine master.* RIGHT: *Covering about 70 acres along the banks of a lake, which was created to aid plant growth, the vineyards produce more than 200 tons of grapes each year.*

WINE PRODUCTION Wine making at Biltmore is a combination of state-of-the-art technology and Old World technique. Although the Winery is one of the leading researchers in viticulture in the East and uses the most advanced equipment, it follows centuries-old practices developed in Europe to produce the finest wines. As a result, its wines have earned a remarkable number of awards—including gold and double-gold medals in prestigious national and international competitions.

The Winery produces 75,000 cases of wine each year in about 15 varieties. The production process begins in the Fermentation Room, where the "must," or crushed grapes, is piped into a series of stainless-steel fermentation tanks, each holding between 3,000 and 5,000 gallons. Grapes for red wine are processed with their skins for flavor and color in computer-controlled rotating tanks for 8 to 21 days, whereas grapes for white wine are fermented without their skins in vertical tanks for up to a month. During fermentation the sugar in the grapes converts to alcohol; when all the sugar is "fermented out," the wine is dry.

The next step is aging, which develops the wine's flavor and bouquet. Because the grapes differ from year to year depending on weather and rainfall, the wine master must determine the proper treatment and aging time for each vintage. Generally, the white wines are aged briefly in the stainless-steel tanks and the red wines are aged for one to two years in oak casks located in the Barrel Room.

The aged wines are bottled in an atmosphere-controlled "clean" room, where the air is filtered and exchanged about every 60 seconds—indicative of the Winery's high standards for purity. Running along an automated assembly line, sterilized bottles are filled, corked, capped, and labeled at a rate of 50 per minute.

Sparkling wines are bottled by hand, a process that visitors can view several times each year. These wines are made by the *méthode champenoise*—the method used for French champagne—which calls for a second fermentation in the bottle to produce the distinctive sparkle. At the end of that two-year process, the bottles are stored neck down on special racks and turned daily. This technique, known as riddling, traps sediment, which is then frozen and disgorged; to replace this "lost" liquid, the bottles are topped with a *dosage*, a special mixture of wine and sugar, before being corked. Riddling racks are on display in the Cellars, where wines and wine barrels are stored in the stone alcoves.

OPPOSITE: *Two white wines—Chardonnay and Sauvignon Blanc—and all the red wines age in casks made of French or American oak; tannin and other natural substances in the wood, which is lightly charred, enhance the wine's flavor.*
ABOVE: *Château Biltmore Chardonnay, which is produced exclusively from grapes grown on the Estate, is one of the more than 100 Biltmore wines that have won awards.*
LEFT: *Sparkling wines, which must ferment in the bottle for two years in a cool, dark place, are stored in the Cellars. After fermentation is complete, the bottles are placed at an inverted angle on a riddling rack.*

TASTING ROOM The spacious Tasting Room, with giant scissor trusses crisscrossing beneath the clerestory ceiling, was originally home to 80 cows. In tribute to its former incarnation, the room was stenciled in a pattern called Victorian Barn, created for Biltmore by John Finney, the artist who restored the elaborately stenciled Victorian-era barns of the British royal family. The design also incorporates the Vanderbilt and Cecil family crests.

In this attractive setting guests are invited to sample different wines at their own pace; for novices and connoisseurs alike, part of the pleasure of wine is discovering new varieties that suit their individual palates. Specially trained hosts are always on hand to assist with tasting techniques, discuss the characteristics of different varietals (a "varietal" wine is named for the dominant grape variety from which it is made), and explain how wine can be used to complement food.

The broad range of Biltmore Estate wines—from the light, delicate Chardonnay Sur Lies to the full-bodied Cardinal's Crest—offers numerous possibilities for enhancing a meal. A classic dry white varietal, such as Sauvignon Blanc, for example, is considered particularly good with seafood. A semi-sweet Chardonnay might be recommended to accompany pasta or poultry. Dry red wines, such as Cabernet Sauvignon, bring out the flavor of meat dishes. Sweet rosés make delicious dessert wines—especially with fruits or chocolate—while sparkling wine can be served with all types of food and at any course.

Adjacent to the Tasting Room—on the site of the former ice cream bar—is a large gift shop with wines, wine glasses and other accoutrements, gourmet foods, and cookbooks.

BELOW: *Known for their record-breaking milk production, Biltmore's pedigreed Jersey cows are shown here around 1939 awaiting their turn in the milking parlor. The barn features a clerestory ceiling, which admits natural light, and scissor trusses, a type of flexible roof support that gives with changes in humidity.*
OPPOSITE: *Stenciled designs, including the Vanderbilt family crest (inset, above), create a festive atmosphere in the Tasting Room, where guests can sample Biltmore's wines.*

BILTMORE HOUSE IS FILLED WITH THOUSANDS OF OBJECTS THAT Mr. Vanderbilt purchased for his new home—including furniture, works of fine and decorative art, books, textiles, and housewares. Listed here, room by room, is an account of the collection on view. As in any residence, housekeeping sometimes requires rearrangement. Biltmore requests the guests' understanding if an object is not found in the room specified.

Non-collection objects such as floral decorations and accessories, candle holders used for *Candlelight Christmas Evenings*, modern seating provided for guest use, and modern fabric table-covers are not listed.

Biltmore House Collections

ENTRANCE HALL

Furniture
Strong chest. Wood and iron. Spain. 17th c.
Humpback chest. Oak and iron. England. 19th c. Elizabethan style.
Armchair. Wood, tooled leather, and metal. Spain. 19th c.
Table. Designer, Richard Morris Hunt (1828–1895). Oak. United States. 19th c. Renaissance style.
Octagon table. Oak. 19th c.
Table. Brass and wood. 19th c.

Decorative Objects
Tall-case clock. Johannes Numan. Mahogany, metal, and paint. Amsterdam, Netherlands. ca. 1750.
Floor lamps. Designer, Richard Morris Hunt (1828–1895). Wrought iron. United States. ca. 1895.
Richard Morris Hunt. Bust. Mary Grant. Marble. Scotland. ca. 1895.
Roger and Angelique on the Hippogriff. Sculpture. Antoine-Louis Barye (1796–1875). Bronze. France. 19th c.
Candelabra. Antoine-Louis Barye (1796–1875). Bronze. France. 19th c.

WINTER GARDEN

Furniture
Settees, armchairs, side chairs, and tables. Perret & Fils et Vibert. Bamboo and rattan. France. 19th c.

Decorative Objects
Oil lamps. Brass. Probably India. 19th c.
Boy Stealing Geese. Fountain sculpture. Karl Bitter (1867–1915). Marble and bronze. United States. 1893–1895.

BILLIARD ROOM

Furniture
Pool and carom tables. Oak and felt. United States. 19th c.
Settees and armchairs. Morant & Co. Leather and oak. England. 1895. Knole style.
High-back side chairs. Leather and wood. 19th c. Flemish style.
Bookcase. Oak. 19th c.
Trestle table with column supports. Wood. France. 19th c.
Cabinet-on-stand. Oak. Germany. 19th c. Late Renaissance style.
Octagon table. Walnut. Italy. 17th c.
Side chairs with leather seat cushions. Stamped leather and oak. Portugal. 17th c.
Cue stands. Wood. 19th c.

Paintings and Prints
Rosita. Painting. Ignacio Zuloaga y Zaboleta (1870–1945). Oil on canvas. Spain. 19th c.
William Henry Vanderbilt Merchant Vessel. Painting. Artist unknown. Oil on canvas. Late 19th–early 20th c.
Prints. After Sir Joshua Reynolds (1723–1792), after George Stubbs (1724–1806), Thomas Atkinson (1817–1889/90), Samuel Cousins (1801–1837), William Dickinson (1746–1767), James Finlayson (1730–1776), Edward Fisher (1722–1785), Valentine Green (1739–1813), John Jones (1745–1797), Thomas Landseer (1798–1880), J. Marchi (1735–1808), James McArdell (1728–1765), John Smith (1652–1742), John Raphael Smith (1752–1812), William Ward (1766–1826), James Watson (1740–1790), William Woollet (1735–1785), and George Vertue (1684–1756). England. 18th and 19th c.

Decorative Objects
Pitcher. Tin-glazed earthenware. England. Late 18th–early 19th c. Delft and Asian influences.
Mask jug. Tin-glazed earthenware. Thuringia, Germany. 19th c. Delft influence.
Tankard with lid. Glazed earthenware and pewter. Netherlands. 18th c.
Tankard with lid. Glazed earthenware. Netherlands. 19th c.
Lidded steins. Villeroy & Boch. Glazed earthenware and pewter. Germany. 19th c.
Lamp. Bronze. 19th c.
Hon. John Francis Amherst Cecil. Photograph. Copy of 20th c. original.
Woodrow Wilson. Photograph. Copy of 20th c. original.
Terrier. Sculpture. Bronze. Berlin, Germany. 19th c. Inscribed "A: Meves. Berlin."

Walking Tiger, Walking Lion, and
Tiger Attacking a Peacock.
Sculpture. Antoine-Louis Barye
(1796–1875). Bronze. France.
19th c.
Standing lamps. Wrought iron.
United States. 19th c.
Globe. C. F. Weber Co. Wood,
paper, and paint. Chicago,
Illinois. 19th c.
Fireplace accessories. Iron
and brass. 19th c.
Billiard game equipment. United
States. 19th and 20th c.
Taxidermic specimens. 19th c.
Rugs. Wool. Kuba region,
East Caucasus. 19th c.

BANQUET HALL

Furniture

Banquet table. Designer,
Richard Morris Hunt
(1828–1895). Oak.
United States. 19th c.
Armchairs and side chairs. Designer,
Richard Morris Hunt
(1828–1895). Walnut and silk.
Italy. 19th c. Baroque
revival style.
Throne chairs. Designer, Richard
Morris Hunt (1828–1895).
Maker, Karl Bitter (1867–1915).
Oak, gilding, and paint. United
States. 19th c.

Tapestries, Flags and Decorative Objects

Tapestries clockwise from the right of the fireplace:
*The Story of Vulcan and Venus:
The Assemblage of the Gods,
The Complaint to Jupiter,
The Dance, Neptune Interceding
for the Lovers,* and *Vulcan Forging
and Spreading the Net.*
Tapestries. Wool, silk,
and metal. Flanders.
ca. 1546–1553.

Flags clockwise from the right of the fireplace:
*Rhode Island, Maryland, New
Hampshire, Massachusetts,
Pennsylvania, New Jersey, Georgia,
South Carolina, Virginia, New
York, Connecticut, Delaware,* and
North Carolina. United States.
Reproductions of late
19th c. originals.
Flag. *World War I Biltmore
Service.* Blue and gold stars.
United States. ca. 1920.

Pennant group above the fireplace; flags clockwise from top:
*Expeditionary Pennant of
Columbus, England, Holland,
New England, Germany, Venice,
Spain, Columbus, Portugal,
China, Japan, Turkey,* and *France.*
United States. Reproductions of
ca. 1895 originals.
Vessels. Brass, copper, and wood.
Netherlands, Spain, and France.
18th–19th c.
Armor. Metal, wood, and fabric.
15th–19th c.
Wine coolers. Brass and copper.
Late 18th–early 19th c.
Candlesticks. Brass. 19th c.
Taxidermic specimens. 19th c.
St. Louis and *St. Joan of Arc.*
Karl Bitter (1867–1915).
Sculpture. Plaster. ca. 1895.
Model for limestone sculpture on
exterior of Biltmore
House staircase tower.
Rug. Wool. Tabriz region,
Persia. 19th c.
Rug. Wool and cotton. Soumak
region, Persia. 19th c.

WINTER GARDEN CORRIDOR

Furniture

Pair of torchères (candle-stands).
Designer, Richard Morris Hunt
(1828–1895). Walnut. Late 19th c.

Decorative Objects

Frieze metopes. Eugene Arrondelle.
Plaster. France. 19th c.
Urn with lion's head designs.
Bronze.

BREAKFAST ROOM

Furniture

Dining table. Mahogany.
United States. ca. 1865.
Daybeds and side chairs. Gilt wood
and silk cut velvet. Probably Italy.
19th c. Baroque style.
Trestle table with column supports.
Wood. ca. 1840–1850.
Draw table with satyr legs. Walnut.
ca. 1845–1855.
Table with melon-bulb legs. Oak.
ca. 1840–1850.
Display cabinet. Brass and glass.
United States. 19th c.

Paintings

Clockwise from above display cabinet:
William Henry Vanderbilt. Painting.
Jared B. Flagg (1820–1899). Oil
on canvas. United States. ca. 1877.
Mrs. Cornelius Vanderbilt. (Sophia
Johnson Vanderbilt). Painting.
Artist unknown. Oil on canvas.
ca. 1860.
Cornelius Vanderbilt. Depicted as a
young man. Painting. Charles
Loring Elliot (1812–1868). Oil on
canvas. United States. ca. 1839.
Mrs. William Henry Vanderbilt.
(Maria Louisa Kissam Vanderbilt).
Painting. George A. Baker (1821–
1880). Oil on canvas. ca. 1880.
Portrait of an unknown man.
Painting. Artist unknown.
Oil on canvas.
Jacob Hand Vanderbilt. Painting.
Charles Loring Elliot (1812–
1868). Oil on canvas. ca. 1839.
Cornelius Vanderbilt. Painting.
Jared B. Flagg (1820–1899). Oil
on canvas. ca. 1876.
Mrs. William Henry Vanderbilt.
(Maria Louisa Kissam Vanderbilt).
Depicted as a young woman.
Painting. Artist unknown.
Oil on canvas. ca. 1840.

Decorative Objects

Dinnerware. Minton. Porcelain.
England. ca. 1896.
Dinnerware. Spode-Copeland.
Porcelain. England. ca. 1896.
Stemware. Baccarat. Crystal.
France. ca. 1897.
Stemware. Webb. Crystal. England.
Early 20th c.
Flatware. Gorham. Stainless steel.
United States. Late 20th c.
Pair of oil lamps. Tiffany & Co.
Silverplate and glass. United
States. ca. 1890.
Table linens. Embroidered linen.
Paris, France, or Ireland. 19th c.
Clock. Marble, glass, and gilded
metal. France. ca. 1788.
Dancing woman and putti group.
Ivory. Europe. 19th c.
Pair of lanterns. Enameled metal.
Italy. 18th c.
Fireplace accessories. Brass. 19th c.
Rug. Wool and cotton. Kurdistan
region, Persia. 19th c.

In brass display cabinet:
Pastoral couple groups. Chelsea.
Porcelain. England. ca. 1752–1758.

*Roger and Angelique on the
Hippogriff, by Antoine-Louis
Barye, 19th century.*
ENTRANCE HALL.

Candlesticks. Meissen. Porcelain.
Germany. 18th c.

Moonlight lustreware in shell
pattern. Wedgwood. Porcelain.
England. 18th c.

Plates. Royal Worcester. Porcelain.
England. Late 19th c.
Japanese influence.

Figures of putti. Ivory. Europe.
19th c.

Serving pieces. Hand-painted
porcelain. 19th c.

Dessert dishes. Minton. Porcelain.
England. 19th c.

SALON

Furniture

Bombé commode. Various woods.
Probably Italy. 18th c. Rococo.

Pair of torchères (candle-stands).
Gilt and painted wood. England.
19th c.

Petit-point screen. Wool, silk, and
gilt wood. France. 19th c.

Double desk. Wood, gilt brass, and
leather. France. 19th c.
Louis XV style.

Side chairs. Cuban mahogany and
caning. England. ca. 1800.
Sheraton style.

Game table. Walnut, acacia, and
ebony. England. 19th c.

Settee and armchairs. Wool tapestry
and walnut. France. 19th c.
Louis XV style.

Pembroke table with claw feet.
Cuban mahogany, rosewood, and
satinwood. England. ca. 1830.

Pembroke table. Cuban mahogany.
England. ca. 1790.

Armchairs. Walnut and velvet.
19th c. Louis XV style.

Table. Papier-mâché, mother-of-
pearl, and gilding. England.
19th c.

Table. Oak. United States. 19th c.
Gothic revival style.

Prints

Portrait prints. Robert Nanteuil
(1630–1678). France.
17th c.

Châteaux prints. Octave de
Rochebrune (1824–1900).
France. 19th c.

Albrecht Dürer (1471–1528) Prints
WEST WALL, TOP TO BOTTOM,
LEFT TO RIGHT:
Ulrich Varnbuler. Woodblock
engraving. Germany. 1522.

The Emperor Maximilian I.
Woodblock engraving.
Germany. 1518–19.

Coat of Arms of Lorenz Staiber.
Woodblock engraving.
Germany. 1520.

Hercules Killing Euryptos.
Woodblock engraving.
Germany. ca. 1496.

The Rhinoceros. Woodblock
engraving. Germany. 1515.

Knight and Lansquenet.
Woodblock engraving.
Germany. ca. 1496.

SOUTHWEST WALL, TOP TO BOTTOM, LEFT
TO RIGHT:
St. Jerome in his Cell. Woodblock
engraving. Germany. 1511.

The Penitent. Woodblock
engraving. Germany. 1510.

St. Francis Receiving the Stigmata.
Woodblock engraving.
Germany. 1503–04.

SOUTHEAST WALL, TOP TO BOTTOM, LEFT
TO RIGHT:
The Adoration of the Magi.
Woodblock engraving.
Germany. 1511.

The Universal Judgment.
Woodblock engraving.
Germany. ca. 1500.

The Holy Kinship with Joachim
and Anna. Woodblock
engraving. Germany. 1511.

EAST WALL, TOP TO BOTTOM,
LEFT TO RIGHT:
The Martyrdom of St. Catherine.
Woodblock engraving.
Germany. ca. 1498.

St. Christopher. Woodblock
engraving. Germany. 1525.

Samson Rending the Lion.
Woodblock engraving.
Germany. ca. 1496.

The Holy Kinship with Angels.
Woodblock engraving.
Germany. 1511.

The Last Supper. Woodblock
engraving. Germany. 1523.

St. Christopher. Woodblock
engraving. Germany. 1511.

Decorative Objects

Clock. Robert Harlow. Mahogany,
brass, and glass. Ashbourne,
England. ca. 1780.

Candelabra with putti. Sèvres.
Bisque porcelain and brass.
France. ca. 1891–1911.

Lamp. United States. 19th c.

Chess set. Ivory. China. 19th c.

Fabric hangings. Silk velvet and
various metals. France. 17th c.

Letter box. Faience ceramic.
France. ca. 1891–1908.
Rococo style.

Pair of candlesticks. Faience ceramic.
France. 18th c. Rococo.

Lion inkwell. Jacques Borrelly.
Faience ceramic. France.
ca. 1749. Rococo.

Napoleon. Bust. Marble. 19th c.

Female bust. Bronze. France. 19th c.

Pair of candlesticks. Antoine-Louis
Barye (1796–1875). Bronze.
France. 19th c.

Louis XVI. Bust. Marble and gilt
wood. France. 19th c.

Male bust, possibly representing a
minor or peasant. Constantin
Emile Meunier (1831–1905).
Bronze. Belgium. 19th c.

Stevedore. Bust. Constantin Emile
Meunier (1831–1905). Bronze.
Belgium. 19th c. Inscribed
"Anvers."

Tall lamps. Wood, glass, and metal.
19th c.

Rug. Wool and cotton. Saraband
region, Persia. 19th c.

Rug. Wool and cotton. Ferahan
region, Persia. 19th c.

MUSIC ROOM

Furniture

Settee and armchairs. Walnut. Italy.
19th c. Baroque revival style.

Monastery table. Wood. Europe.
17th c. style.

Credenza. Walnut. France.
19th c. Gothic style.

Music stand. Wood and gilding. 18th c.

Octagon table. Walnut. Italy. 19th c.

Armchairs. Walnut. Italy. 19th c.
Renaissance style.

Chest-on-stand. Various woods.
Italy. 19th c. Late Renaissance style.

Sideboard. Various woods. Germany.
19th c. Gothic style.

Piano. Steinway and Sons.
United States. Early 20th c.

Side chair. Walnut. Spain. 19th c.

Hobnail chest. Wood and brass.
Spain. 16th c.

Prints

Triumphal Arch of Maximilian.
Woodblock print. Albrecht Dürer
(1471–1528). Germany. Late
18th–early 19th c. copy.

Decorative Objects

Figures of apostles, in cabinet,
left to right from top to bottom:

St. Peter, St. Andrew, St. John, St.
James the Lesser, St. Bartholomew,
St. Simon, St. Jude-Thaddeus, St.
Matthew, St. James the Greater,
St. Thomas, St. Philip, St. Paul.
Designer, Johann Joachim Kändler
(1706–1775). Maker, Meissen.
Porcelain. Germany. 18th c.

Candlesticks. Designer, Johann
Joachim Kändler (1706–1775).
Maker, Meissen. Porcelain.
Germany. 18th c.

Clock. Coward and Company.
Mahogany, brass, other metals,
and glass. England. ca. 1780.

St. John and St. Peter. Sculpture. Gilt
wood and marble. France. 18th c.

Parrots and Eagle Seizing a Serpent.
Sculpture. Antoine-Louis Barye
(1796–1875). Bronze and marble.
France. 19th c.

Male figures, possibly representing
water gods. Sculpture. Bronze.
France. 19th c.

Ritual vessels. Earthenware. China.
Chou Dynasty (1027–256 B.C.).

Lamps. Ceramic and bronze.
Late 19th c.

Candelabra. Iron. 19th c.

Torchères. Wrought iron.
United States. 19th c.

Fireplace accessories. Iron. 19th c.

Rug. Wool and cotton. Khurassan
region, Persia. 19th c.

TAPESTRY GALLERY

Furniture

Dressoirs (dressers). France.
19th c. Gothic style.

Semicircular cabinet. Various
woods. Italy. 17th c.

Vargueño (fall-front cabinet).
Walnut, ivory, metal, gilding, and
paint. Spain. ca. 1600.

Taquillion (base). Walnut, ivory,
metal, gilding, and paint. Spain.
ca. 1600.

Semicircular fold-top table.
England. Early 17th c.

Sofas and club chairs. England.
19th c.

Gateleg tables. Probably Biltmore
Estate Industries. Asheville, North
Carolina. ca. 1906–1917

Stools with scroll feet. Designer,
Richard Morris Hunt (1828–
1895). Walnut. Italy. 19th c.

Table with lion's paw feet. Wood.
19th c. Renaissance revival style.

Side chairs. Stamped-leather, wood,
and metal. Spain or Portugal.
Probably 17th c. Baroque.

Cabinet-on-stand with interior
painted scenes. Ebony and paint.
Flanders. 17th c.

Trestle tables. Walnut and various
other woods. Germany.
ca. 1840. Gothic style.

Chest. France. 19th c. with 15th–
16th c. panels. Gothic style.

Side table. Italy. 19th c.
Draw table. Walnut. 19th c.
with 17th c. components.

Paintings

Ivory and Gold. (Mrs. George
Washington Vanderbilt).
Painting. James McNeill
Whistler (1834–1903). Oil on
canvas. United States. 1902.

Mrs. William Henry Vanderbilt.
(Maria Louisa Kissam Vanderbilt).
Painting. John Singer Sargent
(1856–1925). Oil on canvas.
United States. ca. 1888.

George Washington Vanderbilt.
Painting. John Singer Sargent
(1856–1925). Oil on canvas.
United States. 1895.

Mrs. George Washington Vanderbilt.
(Edith Stuyvesant Dresser
Vanderbilt). Painting. Giovanni
Boldini (1842–1931). Oil on
canvas. Italy. 1911.

Tapestries and Decorative Objects

*The Triumph of the Seven Virtues:
Triumph of Charity, Triumph of
Faith,* and *Triumph of Prudence.*
Tapestries. Wool and silk. Flanders.
ca. 1530.

Vase lamps. Majolica ceramic
and brass. Italy. 19th c.

Lidded bowl. Brass and copper. 19th c.

Collection plate. Brass. 19th c.

Madonna and Child. Icon.
Wood, paint, and gilt metal.
Russia. ca. 1810.

Photographs. Copies of
19th c. originals.

Figure of cat climbing into
kettle. Metal. 19th c.

Box. Various woods. Syria.
Early 20th c.

Benjamin Franklin and *George
Washington.* Busts. Founder,
Ferdinand Barbedienne
(1810–1892), after Jean-Antoine
Houdon (1740–1828). Bronze.
France. 19th c.

Vases. Glazed and painted porcelain.
Japan. ca. 1840–1860.

*Algerian Dromedary, Dromedary and
Rider,* and *Stag at Rest.* Sculpture.
Antoine-Louis Barye (1796–
1875). Bronze. France. 19th c.

Hercules and Antaeus. Sculpture.
Bronze. France. 19th c.

Candelabras. Antoine-Louis Barye
(1796–1875). Bronze. France.
19th c.

Elephant. Sculpture. Bronze.
France. 19th c.

Floor lamps with turtle bases.
Wrought iron. United States.
ca. 1895.

Candlesticks. Bronze. France. 19th c.

Clock. Edmund Card. Ebonized
wood, brass, gilt metal, and glass.
London, England. ca. 1675.

Fireplace accessories. Metal. 19th c.

Rugs. Wool and cotton. Saraband
region, Persia. 19th c.

LIBRARY

Furniture

Settees, armchairs, and side chairs.
Walnut and silk damask. Late
19th c. Baroque style.

Book racks, library steps, large table,
three-legged stools, and stools
with scroll feet. Designer,
Richard Morris Hunt
(1828–1895). Walnut. United
States. Late 19th c.

Bookbinding press. Oak. England.
19th c.

Bench. Metal and velvet.
United States. 19th c.

Two-tiered side tables. Probably
Biltmore Estate Industries. Oak.
Asheville, North Carolina.
ca. 1906–1917.

Painting

The Chariot of Aurora. Painting.
Giovanni Antonio Pellegrini
(1675-1741). Oil on canvas. Italy.
18th c.

Miniature portraits of European
artists. Artist unknown. 19th c.

Decorative Objects and Tapestry

Tapestry. Wool and silk. France. 17th c.

Malby's Terrestrial Globe. Edward
Stanford Geographical Publisher.
Wood, paper, paint, and metal.
London, England. 1899.

Goldfish bowls. Glazed earthenware.
China. Ming Dynasty
(1368–1644).

Floor lamps. Brass and marble.
United States. Late 19th c.

Oil lamps. Ceramic, glass, and brass.
19th c.

George Washington Vanderbilt.
Bust. Mary Grant. Bronze.
Scotland. 1889.

Clock. Metal, gilt wood, and
ebonized wood. Case made in
Spain. Late 17th c. Works
made by Japy Frères. France.
ca. 1880.

Pair of incense burners with
figures. Bronze. 19th c.

Urns. Ceramic. Ginori Brothers.
Florence, Italy. 19th c.
Capodimonte style.

Magnifying glasses. Walnut, glass,
and metal. 19th c.

Candelabrum. Gilt metal and marble.
France. 18th c.

Document repository. Wood, paint,
and gilt. Japan. 18th c.

Crowned eagle lectern. Gilt wood.
Germany. 18th c.

Desk set. Gilt bronze. France.
19th c.

Andirons. Designer, Richard Morris
Hunt (1828–1895). Maker, Karl
Bitter (1867–1915). Iron and
steel. United States. ca. 1895.

Rug. Wool and cotton. Karabagh
region, Persia. 19th c.

**Busts on bookcase in order
from left to right:**

*Cardinal Mazarin. Corneille.
Molière. Montaigne. Cardinal
Richelieu. Colbert. Racine.
Eugene Arrondelle.* Busts.
Plaster. France. 19th c.

GRAND STAIRCASE

Madonna and Child. Tapestry.
Wool. Flanders. Late 15th c.

LOUIS XVI ROOM

Furniture

Bed. Kingwood, rosewood, and brass.
Probably France. Early 20th c.

Chaise longue and side chairs.
Gilt walnut, caning, and silk
damask. France. 19th c.
Louis XVI style.

Roll-top desk. Mahogany, brass, and
leather. France. 19th c.

Pair of console tables. Gilt wood and
marble. France. 19th c.
Louis XVI style.

Center table. Walnut and gilt wood.
France. 19th c. Louis XVI style.

Night table with inlaid classical
figures. England. 18th c.
Neoclassical style.

Night table with marquetry design.
France. Early 19th c.

Kidney-shaped table. Various woods
and gilt brass. France. 19th c.

Cheval mirror. Gilt wood and glass.
France. 19th c. Louis XVI style.

Prints

Prints. School of portraiture
including the artists Pierre
Drevet (1697-1739), and Muller.
France. 19th c.

*Walnut library steps
by Richard Morris Hunt,
late 19th century.* LIBRARY.

Richard Morris Hunt,
by John Singer Sargent, 1895.

SECOND FLOOR LIVING HALL.

Decorative Objects

Toilet bottle. Glass. United States.
  Late 19th–early 20th c.
Hair brush. Ivory and bristles.
  United States. Late 19th c.
Clothes brush. Ivory and bristles.
  United States. Late 19th c.
Comb. Ivory. United States.
  Late 19th c.
Decanters. Cut glass. 19th c.
Vase lamps. France. 19th c.
Clock. Louis Jouard. Gilt
  bronze, enamel, metal, and glass.
  Paris, France. ca. 1750.
Letter opener. Tortoiseshell and
  metal. France. 19th c.
Cassolette (perfume burner). Marble
  and gilt metal. France. 18th c.
Rugs. Aubusson. Wool and cotton.
  France. 19th c.

SECOND FLOOR LIVING HALL

Furniture

Pedestal. Wood. 19th c.
  Gothic revival style.
Armchairs with scroll feet. Oak.
  England. 19th c. Carolean
  revival style.
Settee and barrel-back chair. Fabric
  and wood. England. 19th c.
Pedestal table. Oak. Baroque style.
Desk. Pewter, brass, gilt brass,
  leather, and ebonized wood.
  France. 19th c. Boulle style.
Armchair with ball-and-claw feet.
  Stamped leather and walnut.
  Portugal. 18th c. Rococo.
Settee, armchair, and wingback
  chair. England. 19th c.
Coffer chest. Painted leather, wood,
  and brass. Italy. 19th c.
Chest with carved panels. Oak.
  England. 19th c. Gothic
  revival style.
Travel chest. Wood, ivory, mother-
  of-pearl, brass, enamel. Probably
  Spain. 19th c.
Travel chest stand. Wood. United
  States. Early 20th c.
Arm chairs. Gilded and painted
  pine and caning. Italy. 19th c.
  Venetian revival style.
Gateleg tables. Wood. England or
  United States. Late 19th–early
  20th c.
Table with scrolled stretcher. Wood.
  Spain. 19th c.
Cassone (marriage chest). Gilt wood,
  gesso, and paint. Italy. 19th c.

Paintings

Richard Morris Hunt. Painting.
  John Singer Sargent (1856–1925).
  Oil on canvas. United States. 1895.

Frederick Law Olmsted. Painting.
  John Singer Sargent (1856–1925).
  Oil on canvas. United States. 1895.
The Waltz. Painting. Anders Zorn
  (1860–1920). Oil on canvas.
  Sweden. ca. 1890.
Going to the Opera. (William
  Henry Vanderbilt family).
  Painting. Seymour Guy
  (1824–1875). Oil on canvas.
  United States. 1873.
*The Honorable Mrs. John A. Cecil
  (née Cornelia Vanderbilt).*
  Painting. Nikol Schattenstein
  (1877–1954). Oil on canvas.
  Russia. ca. 1920–1930.
William A. V. Cecil Family.
  Painting. Stone Roberts (1951–).
  Oil on canvas. United States.
  1990–1991.
Genre painting. W. Verhoeven. Oil
  on canvas. Netherlands. 1851.

Decorative Objects

Jean-Louis Ernest Meissonier. Bust.
  Gemilo. Bronze. France. 19th c.
Vases. Porcelain. China. 19th c.
Desk set. Ebonized wood and brass.
  France. 19th c. Boulle style.
Vase oil lamp. Glazed earthenware,
  glass, and metal. 19th c.
Elephant clock. Japy Frères. Bronze,
  gilt metal, and glass.
  France. ca. 1870.
Breton Girl. Sculpture.
  Vallgren. Bronze. 1893.
Incense burner with peacock, and
  ewer with dragon. Satsuma
  painted and glazed earthenware.
  Japan. 18th c.
Wall cases. Gilt wood and glass.
  France. 18th c.
Mah-jongg set. Wood, ivory, and
  metal. Hong Kong. 19th c.
Rug. Wool and cotton. Ferahan
  region, Persia. 19th c.
Rug. Wool. Shirvan region,
  Caucasus. 19th c.

SECOND FLOOR CORRIDOR

Furniture

Cabinets-on-stands. Various woods
  and glass. London, England. 19th c.
  Dutch style.
Caqueteuse chairs. France. 19th c.
  16th c. style.
Commode with lion's paw feet.
  Various woods and marble.
  Italy. 18th c.
Armchairs with rush seats. Various
  woods and rush. Vierlande,
  Germany. 19th c.

Credenza. Oak. 19th c. Gothic style.
Side chairs. Wood and stamped
  leather. Flanders. 18th c.
Table with cabriole legs. Oak. 20th c.
Trestle table. Wood. 19th c.

Paintings and Prints

Engravings.
  William Woollet (1735–1785),
  Sir Robert Strange (1721–1792),
  James Mason (1710–1780),
  Pierre-Charles Canot (1710–1777),
  Francis Vivare (1709–1780), and
  John Charles François (1717–1786).
  England and France. 18th c.
Study of The Christening. Painting.
  Joseph Villegas. Oil on canvas.
  Spain. 1880.

Decorative Objects

Vase. Glazed earthenware and
  ormolu. China. 18th c.
Netsukes, figures, vases, bottles,
  daggers, boxes, and tea caddies.
  Wood, ceramic, lacquer, metal,
  and other materials. Japan and
  China. 18th–19th c.
Molière. Bust. Founder, Ferdinand
  Barbedienne (1810–1892).
  Bronze. France. 19th c.
Demosthenes. Bust. Marble. 19th c.
Female bust. Terra-cotta.
  France. 19th c.
Diana. Bust. Bronze. 19th c.

MR. VANDERBILT'S BEDROOM

Furniture

Tester bed and chairs with figured
  handles. Walnut. Portugal.
  17th c. Baroque.
Settee, daybed, chairs, and dressing
  table with pier glass. Designer,
  Richard Morris Hunt (1828–1895).
  Maker, probably Baumgarten &
  Co. New York. Walnut, glass, and
  brass. ca. 1895.
Tables with twist legs. Wood and
  brass. Portugal. 19th c.
  Baroque style.
Chest-on-chest. Walnut. Italy.
  19th c. Baroque style.
Mirror with crown. Wood, paint,
  gilt, and glass. Portugal. 18th c.
  The initial "M" in the crest
  stands for Queen Maria I, who
  ruled Portugal 1776–1816.
Wall stand. Various woods.
  Italy. 17th c.
Cabinet with textile. Walnut and
  other woods. Italy. Late 17th–
  early 18th c.

Prints
Engravings.

Nicholaus Visscher (1587–1652), Heinrich Aldegrever (ca. 1502–1558), Johan Wierex (1549–1615), Peter Paul Rubens (1577–1640), and Gérard Edelinck (1640–1707). Germany, Netherlands, France, and Flanders. ca. 16th–17th c.

Decorative Objects
Candelabra. Brass. Italy. 19th c.

Desk set. Gilt metal, tortoiseshell, and wood. France. 18th c.

Clock. Metal and wood. Austria. ca. 1650.

Double hourglass. Brass, suede, glass, and sand. 18th c.

Ewers. Bronze. Spain. 19th c.

Urn. Wood. India. 19th c.

Two Dogs Chasing a Partridge. Sculpture. Pierre-Jules Mêne (1818–1871). Bronze. 1847.

Mercury. Sculpture. Bronze. 19th c. Inscribed "AD."

Spartacus. Sculpture. Bronze. France. 19th c. Inscribed "Foyetier 1832."

Friezes, busts, and urns. Eugene Arrondelle. Plaster. France. 19th c.

Covered photograph frame. Tiffany & Co. Brass. United States. Late 19th c.

Candelabra. Brass. Possibly India. 19th c.

Andirons. Metal. 19th c.

Rug. Wool. Tekke tribe, Turkoman. 19th c.

Rug. Wool. Ersari tribe, Turkoman. 19th c.

Rug. Wool. Hamadan region, Persia. 19th c.

OAK SITTING ROOM
Furniture
Cabinet with painted doors. Ebonized and painted wood. Germany. 17th c. Baroque.

Cupboard with figured columns. Oak. Germany. Possibly 19th c. Renaissance style.

Kneehole desk. Various woods, bone, and mother-of-pearl. Spain or Portugal. 18th c.

Chests. Various woods. Italy. 15th c.

Center tables. Walnut and oak. Late 19th c. Renaissance style.

Display cabinet. Ebonized wood, bone, and glass. United States. 19th c.

Side chairs. Walnut. Spain. 19th c.

Cabinet-on-stand. Ebony, various woods, ivory, glass, gilding, paint, metal, and enamel. Antwerp, Belgium. 17th c.

Paintings
Mrs. Benjamin Kissam. (Lucy Hartwell Warren Kissam). Painting. John Singer Sargent (1856–1925). Oil on canvas. ca. 1900.

Mrs. Walter Rathbone Bacon. (Virginia Purdy Bacon). Painting. John Singer Sargent (1856–1925). Oil on canvas. 1896.

Decorative Objects
Goddess of Mercy. Figure. Porcelain. China. 18th c.

Mirrors. Silk velvet, embroidered fabric, glass, and wood. 19th c.

Pair of candelabra. August Nicholas Cain (1821–1904). Bronze. France. Late 19th c.

Coffee set. Porcelain. 19th c.

Pair of candlesticks. Porcelain. Denmark. Late 19th c.

Garniture de Cheminée (group of ceramic vases). Glazed porcelain. China.

Vases. Ceramic. China. 18th and 19th c.

Urn. Tin-glazed earthenware. Italy or Netherlands. 19th c.

Figures. Lacquerware. Japan. 19th c.

Figures of musicians. Ceramic. Japan. 19th c.

Pair of candlesticks in the shape of oil lamps. Bronze. Probably France. 19th c.

The Iron Worker, Man with Glass-Blowing Pipe, and *Hammersmith.* Sculpture. Constantin Emile Meunier (1831–1905). Bronze. Belgium. 19th c.

Bull. Sculpture. Pierre-Jules Mêne (1818–1871). Bronze. 19th c.

Tiger with Bird. Antoine-Louis Barye (1796–1875). Bronze. France. 19th c.

Tea service (in glass cabinet). Sèvres. Porcelain. France. 1888.

Chess set. United States. 19th c.

Decanter and glasses. Crystal. Baccarat. France. ca. 1897. With "GWV" monogram.

Covered urn with dragon spout. Glazed earthenware. China.

Candlesticks. Bronze. United States. 19th c.

Andirons. Metal. 19th c.

Rug. Wool. Konya region, Turkey. 19th c.

Rug. Wool. Kuba region, Caucasus. 19th c.

Rugs. Wool and cotton. Samarkand region, Turkey. 19th c.

MRS. VANDERBILT'S BEDROOM
Furniture
Tester bed. Silk cut-velvet, wood, and metal. United States. 19th c.

Chaise longue, armchairs, and side chairs. France. 19th c. Louis XV style.

Dressing table with mirror. Gilt wood, glass, and silk satin. England. 19th c.

Table. Edwards and Roberts. Ebonized wood, pewter, brass, and tortoiseshell. London, England. Late 19th c. Boulle style.

Bureau. Various woods and Gilt metal. France. 19th c. Louis XV style.

Commode with parquetry. Walnut, various woods, gilt metal, and marble. France. 18th c. Louis XV.

Commode with heart-shaped inlay. Various woods, gilt metal, and marble. Genoa, Italy. 18th c. Rococo.

Cheval mirror. Gilt wood and glass. France. 19th c. Louis XV style.

Night tables. Various woods, marble, and brass. France. 19th c. Directoire style.

Prints
Engravings.

Schmidt, H. Dupont, Pierre Drevet (1697–1739), Roger, and Johan Georg Wille (1715–1808), Paul DelaRoche (1797–1856). Germany and France. 19th c.

Decorative Objects
Urn. Ceramic, metal, and gilt. Vienna, Austria. Second half of 19th c.

Pair of candlesticks. Ginori Brothers. Porcelain. Florence, Italy. 19th c. Capodimonte style.

Pair of candlesticks. Brass. France. 19th c.

Toilet bottles. Silver filigree and glass. France. 19th c.

Photograph frame. Gilt wood and glass. 19th c.

Photographs. Copies of 19th c. originals.

Urn. Majolica ceramic. Italy. 19th c.

Pair of candelabra with figures and flowers. Porcelain and ormolu. France. 18th c.

Clock. Phillipe Barat. Ormolu, porcelain, and glass. France. ca. 1760.

Figure of elephant. Porcelain. England. 19th c.

Compote. Porcelain. Dresden, Germany. 19th c.

Andirons. Brass and iron. 19th c.

Rugs. Savonnerie. Wool. France. 19th c.

STAIRWELL
Prints
Sir Joshua Reynolds (1723–1792), Robert Nanteuil (1630–1678), James Mason (1710–1780), Wilson Lowry (1762–1824), Prior, Francis Vivare (1709–1780), William Woollet (1735–1785), Axel Haig (1835–1921), and Octave de Rochbrune (1824–1900). England and France. 17th–20th c.

NORTH TOWER ROOM
Furniture
Four-poster bed. Mahogany. United States. ca. 1820–1840. American Empire.

Armchairs. Painted wood and cotton sateen. England or United States. Early 19th c.

Chaise longue. Mahogany and cotton sateen. New York. ca. 1820. American Empire.

Pair of octagonal drop-leaf tables. Ebonized wood. England. Late 19th c.

Console table. Wood. England. Late 19th c.

Nesting tables. W. B. Moses and Sons. Painted wood. Washington, D.C. Late 19th c.

Bureau. Edwards & Roberts. Various woods and leather. London, England. Late 19th c. George III style.

Chest of drawers. Satinwood and other woods. United States. ca. 1800–1820. Sheraton style.

Fireplace screen. Wood and embossed paper. England. 19th c.

Prints
Nine Muses with Apollo. Metal-plate engraving. Raphael Urbain Massard (1775–1843) after Jules Romain (1499–1546). 19th c.

Mrs. Musters as Hebe. Mezzotint. C. H. Hodges (1764–1837) after Joshua Reynolds (1723–1792). ca. 1795.

The Right Honorable Lady Jane Halliday. Mezzotint. Valentine Green (1739–1813) after Joshua Reynolds (1723-1792). 1779.

The Infant Hercules. Mezzotint.
William Ward (1766–1826) after
Joshua Reynolds (1723-1792).
ca. 1819.

The Snake in the Grass. Mezzotint.
William Ward (1766–1826) after
Joshua Reynolds (1723–1792).
ca. 1803.

Lady Anne Stanhope. Mezzotint.
James Watson (1740–1790) after
Joshua Reynolds (1723–1792).
ca. 1780.

*Elizabeth, Duchess of Manchester
with Viscount Mandeville as Diana
and Cupid.* Mezzotint. James
Watson (1740–1790) after Joshua
Reynolds (1723-1792). ca. 1780.

Decorative Objects

Figures of boy and girl. Porcelain.
Germany. Late 19th c.
Letter opener. Ivory and silver.
United States. Late 19th c.
Desk set. Ebonized wood, silver,
and glass. France. ca. 1820.
Figure of elephant. Glass. United
States. Late 19th c.
Miniature screen. Brass, glass, gilt, and
painted copper. England. 19th c.
*Mrs. William Jay Scheiffelin and
William Jay Scheiffelin, Jr.*
Photograph. Copy of
ca. 1890 original.
Chestnut urns. Painted tin.
Probably Wales. ca. 1800.
Bowl on stand. Bronze. 19th c.
Photograph frame. Silver and garnet.
United States. Late 19th c.
Miss Lila Vanderbilt. Photograph.
Copy of ca. 1863 original.
Miniature bulldog frame. Metal and
gilt. United States. ca. 1865.
Pan. Sculpture. E. Le Quesne.
Bronze. France. Late 19th c.
Andirons. Cast iron and brass.
United States. ca. 1900.
Clock. Marriot. Ebonized wood,
metals, and glass. London,
England. ca. 1800–1820.
Rug. Wool. Ersari tribe, Turkoman.
Late 19th c.

EARLOM ROOM

Furniture

Tester bed. Mahogany. United
States. ca. 1800–1820.
Armchairs and side chairs. Wood
and cotton velvet. Portugal or
Spain. 19th c.
Center table. Wood, marble, and
brass. France. Early 19th c.
Cheval mirror. Wood and glass.
France. 19th c. Transitional
Rococo/Neoclassical style.

Wardrobe. Various woods.
Netherlands. ca. 1755.
Bureau. Various woods, gilt metal,
and leather. Netherlands. ca. 1755.

Prints

Thomas King and Sophia Baddeley.
Mezzotint. Richard Earlom
(1743–1822) after John Zoffany
(1733–1810). England. ca. 1772.
Game Keepers. Mezzotint. Henry
Birche (pseudonym of Richard
Earlom) after George Stubbs
(1724–1806) and Amos Green
(1735–1807). England. ca. 1790.
Labourers. Mezzotint. Henry Birche
after George Stubbs (1724–1806)
and A. Green (1735–1807).
England. ca. 1790.
A Poultry Market. Mezzotint.
Richard Earlom (1743–1822)
after Frans Snyders (1579–1657).
England. ca. 1783.
A Flower Piece. Mezzotint. Richard
Earlom (1743–1822) after Jan van
Huysum (1682–1749). England.
ca. 1778.
A Fruit Piece. Mezzotint. Richard
Earlom (1743–1822) after Jan van
Huysum (1682–1749). England.
ca. 1781.
A Concert of Birds. Mezzotint.
Richard Earlom (1743–1822)
after Maria de Fiori. England.
ca. 1778.
*Classical Scene with Satyrs,
Animals, and Fowl.* Mezzotint.
Richard Earlom (1743–1822)
after Giovanni Benedetto
Castiglione (ca. 1610–1665).
England. ca. 1781.
Abandonment of Cymo. Mezzotint.
Richard Earlom (1743–1822)
after Giovanni Benedetto
Castiglione (ca. 1610–1665).
England. ca. 1781.

Decorative Objects

Clock with female figure. Bronze,
other metals, marble, and glass.
France. ca. 1800.
Inkwell. Bronze. 19th c.
Figures of satyrs. Bronze. Probably
Italy. 19th c.
*Mrs. William Seward Webb and
Children.* Photograph. Copy of
ca. 1891 original.
Pair of pricket candlesticks. China.
19th c.
Busts. Bronze and marble.
France. ca. 1880.
Andirons. Metal. France. Probably
18th c.
Rug. Wool. Kurdistan region, Iran.
19th c.

RAPHAEL ROOM

Furniture

Sleigh bed. Mahogany. New York,
New York. ca. 1820. Late Federal.
Chest of drawers, pedestal shaving
stand, and washstand. Edwards &
Roberts. Mahogany. London,
England. Late 19th c. Late
Regency or William IV
revival style.
Cupboard secretary. Mahogany.
United States. ca. 1820.
Late Federal.
Sofa. Mahogany and leather. United
States. Late 19th c.
Footstool. Mahogany and leather.
United States. Late 19th c.
Wingback chair. William Phyfe.
Wood and cotton velveteen.
United States. Early 19th c.
Side table. United States.
Late 19th c.

Prints

The Triumph of Galatea. Intaglio
engraving. Joseph C. Richormme
after Raphael (1483–1520).
ca. 1820.
Dispute over the Sacrament (La Disputa).
Metal-plate engraving. Volpato
after Raphael (1483–1520).
ca. 1780.
The Fire in the Borgo. Metal-plate
engraving. Volpato after Raphael
(1483–1520). ca. 1780.
The Transfiguration. Metal-plate
engraving. Raphael Morghen
(1753–1833) after Raphael
(1483–1520). ca. 1800.
The Expulsion of Heliodorus.
Metal-plate engraving. Petrus
Anderloni (1785–1849) after
Raphael (1483–1520). ca. 1830.
*Holy Family with Palm (Vierge aux
Palmiers).* Metal-plate engraving.
Martinet after Raphael
(1483–1520).
The Marriage of the Virgin. Metal-
plate engraving. Richard Steing
after Raphael (1483–1520).
*Virgin and Child with Saints
Elizabeth and John the Baptist.*
Engraving. Auguste Gaspard
Louis Boucher-Desnoyers
(1779–1857) after Raphael
(1483–1520).
*The Virgin of the Veil (Vierge au
Voile).* Engraving. Auguste
Gaspard Louis Boucher-
Desnoyers (1779–1857)
after Raphael (1483–1520).
St. Cecelia. Engraving. Raphael
Urbain Massard (1775–1843)
after Raphael (1483–1520).

The Alba Madonna. Metal-plate
engraving. After Raphael
(1483–1520).
La Belle Jardiniere. Engraving.
Auguste Gaspard Louis Boucher-
Desnoyers (1779–1857)
after Raphael (1483–1520).
*The Madonna of the Chair
(Madonna della Seggiola).*
Intaglio engraving. Raphael
Morghen (1753–1833) after
Raphael (1483–1520). ca. 1810.
Vision of Ezekiel. Engraving. Joseph
Longhi after Raphael
(1483–1520). ca. 1800.

Decorative Objects

Clock. Gustav Becker. Porcelain,
enamel, and gilt metal. Germany.
ca. 1880.
Toilet-bottle covers. Leather.
France. Late 19th c.
Brush and comb set. Ivory. United
States. Late 19th c. With
"WHV" monogram.
Water bottle. Baccarat. Crystal
France. ca. 1897.
Pair of candlesticks. Parian
porcelain, gilt metal, and marble.
England. Second half 19th c.
William K. Vanderbilt, Jr.
Photograph. Copy of ca. 1882
original.
Letter opener. Ivory. Mid to late 19th c.
Desk set. Gilt wood and metal.
United States. 19th c.
Figure of cow. Delft ceramic.
Netherlands. 19th c.
Pair of candlesticks. Probably
Biltmore Industries. Wood.
Asheville, North Carolina.
Early 20th c.
Leslie, C.R. *Memoirs of the Life of
John Constable, ESQ. R.A.*
Composed Chiefly of His
Letters. 2nd ed. London:
Longman, Brown, Green, and
Longmans, 1845.
Fireplace accessories. Metal.
England. ca. 1800-1820.
Rug. Wool and cotton. Anatolia,
Turkey. 19th c.

SOUTH TOWER ROOM

Furniture

Bed. Painted wood and caning.
France. Late 19th c.
Louis XVI style.
Table. Painted wood with
replacement top. France. Late
19th c. Louis XVI style.
Commode. Various woods and
marble. France. Late 19th c.

Cylinder bureau. Satinwood and
other woods. England. ca. 1910.
George III style.
Chest of drawers. Wood, marble,
and brass. France. 19th c.
Pembroke table. Mahogany.
England. ca. 1790.
Center table. Wood, marble, and
brass. France. Late 19th c.
Louis XVI style.
Arm chairs and side chairs with
caned seats. Cuban mahogany
and caning. England. ca. 1800.
Sheraton style.
Side chairs with cabriole legs. Various
woods. England. Late 19th c.
Two-tiered end table. Walnut.
United States. ca. 1900.
Sofa and occasional chair. Printed
cotton and wood. Howard and
Company. London, England.
ca. 1895.
Slipper chair. Cotton sateen and
wood. England. Late 19th c.

Prints
*Marie Antoinette de Lorraine
d'Autriche, Reine de France.*
Hand-colored engraving. Roger
after Rosslim le Suedois. France.
ca. 1790.
Louis XVI. Hand-colored engraving.
Charles Bervic (1756–1822) after
Callet (1741–1823). ca. 1790.
*Louis Alexandre de Bourbon,
Comte de Toulouse, Admiral de
France.* Mezzotint. Pierre Drevet
(1697–1739) after Hyacinthe
Rigaud (1659–1743). France.
ca. 1750.
*Claude Louis Hector, Duc de
Villars.* Mezzotint. Pierre Drevet
(1697–1739) after Hyacinthe
Rigaud (1659–1743). ca. 1750.

Decorative Objects
Perfume bottle set. Baccarat.
Crystal, gilt, and bronze.
France. ca. 1890.
Pair of candlesticks. Ormolu and
porcelain. France. Mid 18th c.
Group of man, woman, and child.
Unglazed and painted porcelain.
Thuringia, Germany. Late 19th c.
Pair of candlesticks. Brass. France.
19th c. Louis XIV style.
Miniature table and chairs.
Porcelain. France. 19th c.
Rococo style.
Figure of dove. Rose quartz.
Probably China. 19th c.
Photograph. Copy of ca. 1882
original.

Andirons. Metal. France.
Probably 18th c.
Rug. Aubusson. Wool, cotton, and
silk. France. 19th c.

BATHROOM
Towel rack. Mahogany. 19th c.
Toilet chair. Wood and caning. 19th c.
Towels. Embroidered linen. 19th c.

WATSON ROOM
Furniture
Pair of twin beds. Mahogany and
boxwood. England. ca. 1900.
Neoclassical style.
Bedside cabinet. Mahogany and
boxwood. England. Early 20th c.
Neoclassical style.
Wardrobe. Mahogany. England.
Late 19th–early 20th c.
Neoclassical style.
Wing-back easy chair. Mahogany
frame with linen slip-cover.
United States. ca. 1795–1805.
Center table. Walnut and leather.
England. ca. 1800–1850.
Regency style.
Washstand. Mahogany, satinwood,
marble, ceramic tile, and brass.
Probably England. Late 19th–early
20th century. Hepplewhite style.
Daybed. Oak frame with cotton/linen
slip-cover. Probably United States.
ca. 1890–1910.
Tambour-top desk. Mahogany,
satinwood, and brass. England.
Late 19th–early 20th century.
Hepplewhite style.
Pair of side chairs. Mahogany and
printed cotton. Probably England
or United States. 19th century.
Neoclassical style.

Decorative Objects
Lamp. Ceramic, wood, and brass.
Japan. ca. 1900–1911.
Ceramic basket. Porcelain.
Italy. ca. 1920–1930.
Figure of seated man with dog.
Bisque porcelain and gilt brass.
France. ca. 1850–1900.
Round dish. Porcelain. Italy. 19th c.
Female bust. Bronze and marble.
Italy. ca. 1875–1900.
Vase. Glass and sterling silver.
United States. Louis Comfort
Tiffany. 1895.
Toilet porcelain. Minton. England.
ca. 1895. "GWV" monogram.
Hairbrush. Metal and bristles. United
States. Late 19th–early 20th c.

Toilet bottle covers. Leather. France.
Late 19th–early 20th c.
Carafe. Purple glass. England,
possibly Bristol. ca. 1900.
Towels. Linen. Italy. Purchased 1999.
Pair of bookends. Leather, gilding,
metal, and fabric. ca. 1890.
Pair of vases. Purple glass. Bohemia.
ca. 1850–1900.
Inkstand. Porcelain and gilt metal.
China and France. 19th c. The
early 19th c. Chinese porcelain
parts were combined with French
gilt bronze in the late 19th c.
Paper knife. Ivory and silver.
ca. 1900. "GV" monogram.
Fountain pen. Ivory, metal, and horn.
United States. ca. 1890.
Round box. Papier-mache and paint.
England. ca. 1810–1815.
Miniature portrait on lid with
inscription inside lid reading
"The expecting beauty."
Mercury. Bust. Bronze. Rome, Italy.
ca. 1850–1900.
Wastebasket. Wicker. United States.
Late 19th–early 20th c.
Rug. Wool and cotton. Ferahan
region, Persia. ca. 1875–1900.
Rug. Wool and cotton. Sarabend
region, Persia. 19th c.

In bathroom:
Soap dish. Metal. United States.
Late 19th–early 20th c.

Prints

North Wall, over the mantel:
Anne Elliott. Mezzotint.
James Watson (1740–1790)
after Tilly Kettle (1735–1786).
England. 18th c.
Mrs. Abingdon. Mezzotint. James
Watson (1740–1790) after Sir
Joshua Reynolds (1723–1792).
England. 18th c.

East Wall:
Margaret, Lady Bingham.
James Watson (1740–1790) after
Angelica Kauffman (1740–1807).
England. 1775.
*The Right Honorable Lady
Molineux.* Mezzotint. James
Watson (1740–1790) after Sir
Joshua Reynolds (1723–1792).
England. 1770.
Miss Mary Cunliffe. Mezzotint.
James Watson (1740–1790)
after Francis Cotes (1726–1770).
England. 18th c.
Lady Susan O'Brien. Mezzotint. James
Watson (1740–1790)
after Francis Cotes (1726–1770).
England. 1772.

**H.R.H., The Duchess
of Cumberland,** *engraved
by James Watson,* 1773.
WATSON ROOM.

South Wall, over the wardrobe:
Frances, Lady Bridges. Mezzotint.
James Watson (1740–1790) after
Francis Cotes. England. 1768.

South Wall, in window alcove:
HRH the Duchess of Cumberland. Mezzotint. James Watson (1740–
1790) after Sir Joshua Reynolds
(1723–1792). England. 1773.

West Wall, either side of windows:
Polly Jones. Mezzotint. James Watson
(1740–1790) after Reed.
England. 18th c.

Miss Julia Bosville. Mezzotint.
James Watson (1740–1790) after
Sir Joshua Reynolds (1723–1792).
England. 1775.

North Wall, in window alcove:
Miss Annabelle Blake. Mezzotint.
James Watson (1740–1790) after
Sir Joshua Reynolds (1723–1792).
England. 18th c.

Books
Bible. *The New Testament of Our Lord
and Savior Jesus Christ.* London:
Longman, Green, Longman,
Roberts, and Green, 1865.
Ruskin, John. *The Crown of Wild
Olive.* Edition de Luxe. Boston:
Frederick J. Quinby Company, n.d.
Ruskin, John. *Deucalion.* Edition de
Luxe. Boston: Frederick J. Quinby
Company, n.d.
Ruskin, John. *Fors Clavigera: Letters to
the Workmen and Labourers of Great
Britain.* Edition de Luxe.
2 vols. Boston: Frederick J. Quinby
Company, n.d.
Ruskin, John. *Hortus Inclusus:
In Montibus Sanctis-Cœli Enarrant.*
Edition de Luxe. Boston:
Frederick J. Quinby Company, n.d.
Ruskin, John. *Modern Painters.*
Edition de Luxe. 2 vols. Boston:
Frederick J. Quinby Company, n.d.
Ruskin, John. *The Seven Lamps of
Architecture: Lectures on
Architecture and Painting.*
Edition de Luxe. Boston:
Frederick J. Quinby Company, n.d.
Ruskin, John. *The Two Paths.*
Edition de Luxe. Boston:
Frederick J. Quinby Company, n.d.

Framed Family Photographs
(All photographs are copies of originals
in the Biltmore Estate archives; they are
framed in contemporary frames.)

*Lila Vanderbilt Webb with children Fred-
erica and James Watson Webb*
Hamilton Twombly (young boy)
Alice Twombly (young girl)

**Mahogany and painted
chest-on-cabinet, late
19th century.**
VAN DYCK ROOM.

VAN DYCK ROOM
Furniture
Bed. Walnut. France, possibly Provin-
cial. ca. 1840–1850.
Empire style.
Night table. Mahogany and various
woods. England. 19th c.
Chest-on-cabinet. Mahogany and
paint. England. Late 19th c.
George III style with painted
scenes inspired by Angelica
Kauffman.
Cheval mirror. Mahogany, brass,
glass. England. Mid–19th c.
Regency style.
Dressing table with triple mirror.
Mahogany. United States. Late
19th c. Colonial Revival style.
Tripod table with oval top.
Satinwood, rosewood, mahogany,
and maple. Probably United
States. Probably Biltmore Estate
Industries. ca. 1900.
Daybed. Oak and cotton damask.
A. H. Davenport. Boston,
Massachusetts. ca. 1890–1900.
Slipper chair. Walnut and cotton
damask. Probably United States
ca. 1890–1900.
Table with center drawer.
Mahogany. Probably United
States. Late 19th c.
Desk. Mahogany, other woods,
felt, and brass. United States.
ca. 1795–1800. Sheraton style.
Washstand. Mahogany, marble,
and ceramic tile. United States.
Late 19th c.
Pair of side chairs. Mahogany,
beech, and cane. Probably
England. 19th c. Regency.

Decorative Objects
Lamp. Ceramic, brass, and wood. Late
19th–early 20th c.
Dish. Papier-mâché and lacquer. Eng-
land. ca. 1910. Japanese style.
Toilet bottle covers. Leather.
France. Late 19th–early 20th c.
Lotion bottle. Glass and paint.
United States. ca. 1920.
Powder jar. Glass and sterling silver.
Probably England. ca. 1925.
Pincushion. Wood, enamel, paint,
and silk. China and England.
Late 19th c. The base is an
English wine coaster, with a
Chinese silk cushion added.
Hairbrush. Metal and bristles. United
States. Late 19th–early 20th c.

Pair of vases. Satsuma earthenware.
Japan. ca. 1880. Painted with
parades of realistic insects. From
the collection of George Vander-
bilt's father, William H. Vanderbilt,
at 640 Fifth Ave., New York.
Bookends. Oak and paint.
United States. ca. 1920.
Pair of blue and white candlesticks.
Tin-glazed earthenware.
Holland. ca. 1850–1900.
Paper knife. Tortoiseshell and gilt
brass. France. ca. 1880–1890.
Inkwell. Ceramic. Late 19th–early
20th c.
Wastebasket. Wicker. United States.
Late 19th–early 20th c.
Figure of boy and girl. J. P. Danhofer,
Hochst factory. Ceramic.
Germany. Second half of 18th c.
Figure of girl in pink dress.
Hochst factory. Ceramic.
Germany. ca. 1763–1796.
Toilet porcelain. Minton. England.
ca. 1895. "GWV" monogram.
Towel rack. Mahogany. United
States. Late 19th–early 20th c.
Towels. Linen. Italy. Purchased 1999.
Rug. Wool. Qashgai region,
Persia. 19th c.
Rug. Wool. Kazak district,
Caucasus. Late 19th c.
Soap dish. Metal. United States.
Late 19th–early 20th c.

Prints
North Wall:
Rubens' Sons. Mezzotint. Johann
Peter Pichler (1765–1807) after
Anthony Van Dyck (1599–1641).
England. 1802.
Rachel, Countess of Southampton.
Mezzotint. James MacArdell
(1728–1765), after Anthony
Van Dyck (1599–1641).
England. 1758.

East Wall, over mantel
*Henrietta Maria, Queen of Charles I,
and His Two Sons.* Mezzotint.
Sir Robert Strange (1721–1792),
after Anthony Van Dyck
(1599–1641). England. 1784.
Charles I. Mezzotint. Sir Robert
Strange (1721–1792), after
Anthony Van Dyck (1599–1641).
England. ca. 1784.

South Wall
*George, Duke of Buckingham, and
His Brother.* Mezzotint. James
MacArdell (1728–1765), after
Anthony Van Dyck (1599–1641).
England. 18th c.

Children of Charles I. Mezzotint.
Q. Purcell, after Anthony Van
Dyck (1599–1641). England.
18th c.

South Wall, window alcove:
James, Duke of Richmond. Mezzotint.
Richard Earlom (1743–1822)
after Anthony Van Dyck
(1599–1641). England. 1773.

North Wall, window alcove:
*Lord John and Lord Bernard Stuart,
Sons of Esme, Duke of Lenox.*
Mezzotint. James MacArdell
(1728–1765), after Anthony
Van Dyck (1599–1641).
England. 18th c.

Books
Blake, H.G.O., ed. *Early Spring in
Massachusetts from the Journal
of Henry David Thoreau.* Riverside
ed. Vol. V. Boston: Houghton,
Mifflin and Co., 1894.

Browning, Elizabeth Barrett. *Hitherto
Unpublished Poems and Stories with
an Inedited Autobiography.* 2 vols.
Boston: Printed exclusively for
members of the Bibliophile
Society, 1914.

Dickens, Mary Angela, ed.
The Letters of Charles Dickens.
3 vols. London: Chapman
and Hall…, 1880–1882.

D'Orléans, Duchesse. *Secret Memoirs
of the Court of Louis XIV and of the
Regency.* Grand Luxe ed. Boston,
C.H. Simonds and Company,
Colonial Press, n.d.

Saintsbury, George. *The Writings of
Prosper Mérimée…* Imperial ed.
Translated by William M. Arnold,
Olive Edwards Palmer, Emily
Mary Waller. New York:
Frank S. Holby, 1906.

Tolstoy, Count Leo N. *Death of Iván
Ilich.* Edited and Translated by
Leo Wiener. London: G.J. Howel
& Co…, 1905.

Tolstoy, Count Leo N. *The Kingdom
of God is Within You.* Edited and
Translated by Leo Wiener.
London: G.J. Howel & Co…, 1905.

Tolstoy, Count Leo N. *Walk in
the Light While Ye Have Light.*
Edited and Translated by
Leo Wiener. London:
G.J. Howel & Co…, 1905.

Tolstoy, Count Leo N. *What Shall We
Do Then?* Edited and Translated
by Leo Wiener. London:
G.J. Howel & Co…, 1905.

Family Photographs
(All photographs are copies of originals
in the Biltmore Estate archives; they are
framed in contemporary frames.)

On bedside table:
Emily Vanderbilt (young girl)
Emily and Florence Vanderbilt
(young girls)

On dressing table:
William K. Vanderbilt (as a teenager)
Cornelius Vanderbilt II (as a teenager)

On side table:
Gertrude Vanderbilt (young girl)
Frederick Vanderbilt (young man)
Lila Vanderbilt (young woman)
Consuelo Vanderbilt (girl)

MORLAND ROOM
Furniture
Bed. Rosewood. United States.
19th c. Rococo Revival style.
Bed half-tester. Rosewood and
cotton sateen. United States.
19th c. Rococo Revival style.
Bed draperies. Heather Allen.
Cotton and fabric inks. Asheville,
North Carolina. 1998–1999.
Hand-painted reproductions of
early 19th c. hand-painted Indian
textiles used as bed draperies in
this room c. 1900.
Pair of small bombe-shaped cabinets.
Walnut and other woods. Holland.
19th c. Rococo Style.
Dressing stand with mirror.
Mahogany and glass. United
States. Early 20th c.
Armoire. Oak. Normandy, France.
18th c. Rococo.
Daybed. Oak and linen.
A. H. Davenport. Boston,
Massachusetts. ca. 1890–1900.
Arm chair. Oak and linen. Probably
United States. ca. 1890–1900.
Slipper chair. Howard & Sons.
Mahogany and linen. England. ca.
1890–1900.
Chest-of-drawers. Mahogany and
other woods. England. 19th c.
Rococo style.
Desk. Walnut. France. ca. 1860.
Rococo style.
Side chair. Walnut and velvet.
Spain or Portugal. Late 19th c.

Decorative Objects
Jade tree. Stone (including
turquoise), coral, enamel,
metal, other materials. China.
ca. 1900–1930.
Pair of parrot figurines. Glazed
ceramic. China. Early 20th c.

Lidded jar. Turquoise glass.
France. ca. 1920–1930.
Toilet bottle (tea caddy). Porcelain.
China. Early 19th c.
Pin cushion. Sterling silver and
velvet. United States.
ca. 1900–1914.
Vase. Glazed porcelain. China.
Late 19th–early 20th c.
Sang-de-boeuf style glaze.
Lamp. Ceramic, wood, and brass.
China and United States.
ca. 1930. Chinese vase
converted to an electrified lamp.
Inkwell in form of an elephant.
Bronze, glass, and enamel.
Staffordshire, England.
ca. 1870–1884.
Paper knife. Tortoiseshell and gilt
brass. Paris, France. ca. 1900.
Female figure. Sculpture. Bronze
and marble. Italy. Early 20th c.
Candelabrum with screen. Gilt brass
and silk. France. Late 19th c.
Rococo style.
Letter box. Wood and lacquer.
Probably England. c. 1900.
Japanese style.
Wastebasket. Wicker. United States.
Late 19th–early 20th c.
Rug. Wool. Morocco. ca. 1875–1900.
Rug. Wool. Kazak region,
Caucasus. ca. 1875–1900.
Soap dish. Metal. United States. Late
19th–early 20th c.

Prints
Over the mantel:
The Hard Bargain. Mezzotint.
William Ward (1766–1826) after
George Morland (1762/3–1804).
England. 1803.
The Last Litter. Mezzotint.
William Ward (1766–1826) after
George Morland (1762/3–804).
England. 1803.

East Wall:
The Shepherds. Mezzotint.
William Ward (1766–1826) after
George Morland (1762/3–1804).
England. 1806.
Children Bird-Nesting. Mezzotint.
William Ward (1766–1826) after
George Morland (1762/3–1804).
England. 1789.

North Wall, in window alcove:
Contemplation. Mezzotint.
William Ward (1766–1826) after
George Morland (1762/3–1804).
England. 1786.

**West Wall, either side
of the windows:**
Setters. Mezzotint. Samuel William
Reynolds, Sr. (1773–1835) after
George Morland (1762/3–1804).
England. 1798.
Setters. Mezzotint. William Ward
(1766–1826) after George
Morland (1762/3–1804).
England. 1806.

Books
Dickens, Charles. *Works of Charles
Dickens: Little Dorrit.* Household
ed. Vol. IV. New York: Sheldon
and Company…, 1863.
Dickens, Charles. *Works of Charles
Dickens: Martin Chuzzlewit.*
Household ed. 2 vols. New York:
Sheldon and Company…, 1862.
Iles, George, ed. *The Naturalist as
Interpreter and Seer.* Little
Masterpieces of Science Series.
New York: Doubleday, Page &
Company, 1902.
Lobetira, Vasco. *Amadis of Gaul.*
Trans. by Robert Southey.
Vols. I & II. London: Printed by
N. Biggs…, for T.N. Longman
and O. Rees…, 1803.
Scott, Sir Walter, Bart. *The Waverley
Novels.* Vols. 1 & 2. Edinburgh:
Adam and Charles Black, 1860.
Southey, Robert. *Omniana: or Horæ
Otiosiores.* Vol. 1. London:
Printed for Longman, Hurst, Rees,
Orme and Brown…, 1812.

Family Photographs
(All photographs are copies of originals
in the Biltmore Estate archives; they are
framed in contemporary frames.)
William H. Vanderbilt
Maria Louisa Kissam Vanderbilt

MADONNA ROOM
Furniture
Daybed. Oak and cotton damask.
A. H. Davenport. Boston,
Massachusetts. ca. 1890–1900.
Center table. Rosewood and marble.
United States. Mid-19th c.
Renaissance Revival style.
Arm chair. Walnut, velvet, and
cotton. Italy. Late 19th c. Italian
Renaissance style.
Bed. Rosewood. United States.
ca. 1860–1880. Renaissance
Revival style.

Cassone (marriage chest). Probably Herter Brothers. Oak. United States. ca. 1880–1890. Italian Renaissance style. Probably from the collection of George Vanderbilt's father, William H. Vanderbilt, at 640 Fifth Ave., New York.

Chest-of-drawers. Rosewood, burr maple or birch, mahogany, and gilt wood. Italy. ca. 1840.

Desk. Oak. United States. Late 19th c. Renaissance Revival style.

Pair of side chairs. Walnut and velvet. Probably England. Late 19th c. Style of ca. 1660 Carolean furniture.

Cupboard. Oak and ebonized fruitwood. 19th c. Baroque Revival style.

Washstand. Oak and marble. United States. Late 19th c. Renaissance Revival style.

Decorative Objects

Pair of candlesticks. Delft soft-paste porcelain. Delft, Holland. ca. 1890.

Bracket clock. Case by Edward Burgess. Ebonized wood, metal, and glass. England. Case ca. 1685–1700. Works not original.

Figure of boy with goat. Sculpture. Boxwood. Italy. 19th century.

Photo album. Gold-tooled Morocco leather, metal, and paper board. 19th century.

Dish. Brass and enamel. India. ca. 1890. Decorated in the Florentine manner.

Lamp (vase converted to electrified lamp). Vase possibly by Tiffany & Co. Ceramic, enamel, and metal. United States. ca. 1895. Persian-influenced design.

Collapsible bookends. Biltmore Estate Industries. Oak and metal. Asheville, North Carolina. ca. 1906–1917.

Inkwell. Majolica ceramic. Italy, possibly Florence. 19th c.

Pair of candlesticks. Poryphory and gilt brass. France. ca. 1840.

Paper knife. Tortoiseshell and silver. Italy. Late 19th c. "GWV" monogram.

Christ Bearing His Cross. Framed plaque. Niello (type of engraved silver) and ebonized wood. Italy. 17th c. Paper labe (probably 19th c.) on reverse reads "Old Italian niello–original silver plate 'Christ Bearing His Cross' from the collection of the Marchesi Jacopo Durezzo at Genoa."

Wastebasket. Wicker. United States. Late 19th–early 20th c.

Rug. Wool and cotton. Mashad district, Persia (eastern Iran). 19th c.

Soap dish. Metal. United States. Late 19th–early 20th c.

Prints

Clockwise around room, beginning on North Wall near door from Morland Room:

Holy Family. Engraving. Raphael Morghen (1753–1843) after Andreas Vannuchius. Italy. Late 18th–early 19th c.

La Madonna d. San Sisto di Rafaele. Engraving. Friedrich Muller (1752–1825), after Raphael (1483–1520). Germany. Late 18th–early 19th c.

The Immaculate Conception. Engraving. Achille-Desire Lefevre (1798–1864) after Bartolome Murillo (1617–1682). France. 19th c.

Madonna della Scala. Engraving. Toschi after Antonio Allegri Corregio (ca. 1489–1534). Italy. Probably 19th c.

The Madonna of the Burgomaster. Engraving. Moritz Steinla (1791–1858) after Hans Holbein the Younger (1497/8–1543). Germany. 19th c.

Unknown title (Madonna with sleeping child). Engraving. Gregorio Cleter (1831–?) after Carlos Dolci (1616–1686). Italy. 19th c.

The Assumption of the Virgin. Engraving. Natale Schiavone (1777–1858) after Titian (ca. 1487–1576). Italy. Late 18th–mid 19th c.

La Sibylle de Cumes. Engraving. Marcantonio Raimondi (ca. 1480– ca. 1534). Italy. Late 15th–early 16th c.

Repose in Egypt. Engraving. Lucas van Leyden (1494–1533). Holland. Early 16th c.

Augustus and the Sibyl. Engraving. Master E. S. (worked 1440– 1467). Germany. 15th c.

The Return of the Prodigal Son. Engraving. Lucas van Leyden (1494–1533). Holland. Early 16th c.

Pieta. Engraving. Caprarola. Probably Italy. 1597.

Christ on the Cross. Engraving. Martin Schongauer (ca. 1430–1491). Germany. 15th c.

The Mocking of Christ. Engraving. Israhel von Meckenem. Germany. Late 15th c.

Christ Arising from the Tomb. Engraving. Israhel von Meckenem. Germany. Late 15th c.

Madonna in the Clouds. Engraving. Marcantonio Raimondi (ca. 1480–ca. 1534). Italy. Late 15th–early 16th c.

Books

Blake, H.G.O., ed. *The Writings of H. D. Thoreau.* Vol. VII, *Autumn from the Journal of Henry David Thoreau.* Riverside ed. Boston: Houghton, Mifflin and Company, 1894.

Browning, Robert. *The Poetical Works of Robert Browning.* Vols. VII, VIII, XIII. London: Smith, Elder, and Company, 1888–1889.

Gorky, Maxim. *The Man Who Was Afraid.* Translated by Herman Bernstein. Popular ed. London: T. Fisher Unwin, 1905.

Gorky, Maxim. *Orloff and His Wife: Tales of the Barefoot Brigade.* Translated by Isabel F. Hapgood. Authorized ed. NY: Charles Scribner's Sons, 1901.

Gorky, Maxim. *The Outcasts and Other Stories.* London: T. Fisher Unwin, 1902.

Gorky, Maxim. *The Spy.* London: Duckworth and Company…, 1908.

Scott, Sir Walter, Bart. *The Waverley Novels.* Vol. XX, *The Abbot; Being the Sequel to the Monastery.* Edinburgh: Adam and Charles Black, 1860.

Scott, Sir Walter, Bart. *The Waverley Novels.* Vol. XXV, *The Pirate.* Edinburgh: Adam and Charles Black, 1860.

Thackeray, William Makepeace. *Vanity Fair: A Novel Without A Hero.* Collection of British Authors Series. 3 vols. Copyright ed. Leipzig: Bernhard Tauchnitz, 1848.

Thoreau, Henry David. *Cape Cod.* Boston: Houghton, Mifflin and Company, 1894.

Family Photographs

(All photographs are copies of originals in the Biltmore Estate archives; they are framed in contemporary frames.)

Hamilton Twombly, Sr. (man)
Cornelius Vanderbilt II (young man)
Florence, Ruth, and Alice Twombly (three children)
Florence Twombly with her children Florence, Ruth, and Alice

CORRIDOR

right to left, proceeding from the Madonna Room toward the Grand Staircase

Prints

John, Duke of Marlborough. Mezzotint. John Smith (1652–1743), after Sir Godfrey Kneller (ca. 1649–1723). England. ca. 1705.

Zachariah Mudge. Mezzotint. James Watson (1740–1790), after Sir Joshua Reynolds (1723–1792). England. 18th c.

Catherine, Lady Copley. Mezzotint. John Smith (1652–1743), after Sir Godfrey Kneller (ca. 1649– 1723). England. 1697.

Charles, Lord Euston. Mezzotint. John Smith (1652–1743), after Sir Godfrey Kneller (ca. 1649–1723). England. 1689.

Sophia Dorothea, Princess Royal of Prussia. Mezzotint. John Smith (1652–1743), after Johann Hirseman (1672–1750). England. 1706.

A Lady. Mezzotint. Purcell (also known as Charles Corbutt) after Titian (ca. 1487–1576). England. 18th c.

Lady Selina Hastings. Mezzotint. Richard Houston (1721–1775), after Sir Joshua Reynolds (1723–1792). England. 18th c.

Giuseppi Marchi. Mezzotint. John Spilsbury (1730–1795), after Sir Joshua Reynolds (1723–1792). England. 1761.

Sara, Duchess of Marlborough. Mezzotint. John Smith (1652–1743), after Sir Godfrey Kneller (ca. 1649–1723). England. 1705.

Mr. Greville Verney. Mezzotint. Robert Williams (worked 1680–1704), after Michael Dahl (1659–1743). England. Late 17th–early 18th c.

Philip Dormer Stanhope, Earl of Chesterfield. Mezzotint. John Simon (1675–1754), after William Hoare (ca. 1707–1792). England. 18th c.

Catherine Chambers. Mezzotint. James MacArdell (1728–1765), after Sir Joshua Reynolds (1723–1792). England. 1756.

John Smith. Mezzotint. John Smith (1652–1743), after Sir Godfrey Kneller (ca. 1649–1723). England. 1716.

Lady Fortescue. Mezzotint. James MacArdell (1728–1765), after Sir Joshua Reynolds (1723–1792). England. 18th c.

Mrs. Fitzwilliam. Mezzotint. John Raphael Smith (1752–1812), after himself. England. 1777.

Princess Sophia. Mezzotint. John Smith (1652–1743), after unknown painter. England. 1706.

John, Earl of Mulgrave. Mezzotint. John Smith (1652–1743), after Sir Godfrey Kneller (ca. 1649–1723). England. Early 18th c.

Jane, Duchess of Gordon. Mezzotint. William Dickinson (1746–1823) after Sir Joshua Reynolds (1723–1792). England. 1796.

Miss Harriet Powel. Mezzotint and drypoint etching. John Raphael Smith (1752–1812), possibly after Matthew William Peters (1742–1814). England. 1776.

The Right Hon. Charles Montague. Mezzotint. John Smith (1652–1743), after Sir Godfrey Kneller (ca. 1649–1723). England. Early 18th c.

Richard, Lord Clifford, and Lady Jane Boyle, His Sister. Mezzotint. John Smith (1652–1743), after Sir Godfrey Kneller (ca. 1649–1723). England. Early 18th c.

William, Duke of Gloucester. Mezzotint. John Smith (1652–1743), after Sir Godfrey Kneller (ca. 1649–1723). England. ca. 1699.

Hon. Elizabeth Barrington. Mezzotint. Richard Houston (1721–1775), after Sir Joshua Reynolds (1723–1792). England. 1758.

THIRD FLOOR STAIRCASE LANDING

Cabinet. Oak. Probably Italy. 19th c. Renaissance style.

Prints. England. 19th c.

SECOND FLOOR STAIRCASE LANDING

Bookcase cabinet with clock. Oak and glass. France, probably Brittany or Normandy. Third quarter 18th c. Provincial Louis XV style.

Clock mounted in bookcase cabinet. Brass and other metals. Netherlands. ca. 1860.

Male bust. A. C. Belleuse. Bronze. France. 19th c.

Pedestal. Wood. 19th c. Gothic revival style.

Julius Caesar and *Augustus Caesar*. Busts. Marble. 19th c.

Prints. Axel Herman Haig (1838–1921). Sweden. 19th c.

HALLWAY OUTSIDE SHERATON ROOM

Wall plaques. Wedgwood. Basaltes ware and gilt wood. England. 19th c.

Watercolors. Lady William Cecil (1857–1919). England. Early 20th c.

SHERATON ROOM

Furniture

Tester bed. Painted satinwood. England. 19th c.

Wardrobe. Various woods. England. Late 19th c.

Double writing desk. Edwards & Roberts. Various woods, brass, and leather. London, England. Late 19th c.

Side chair. Satinwood and fabric. England. 19th c.

Sideboard. Edwards & Roberts. Mahogany. London, England. Late 19th c.

Washstand. Painted satinwood and marble. England. Late 19th c.

Sofa, side chairs, and benches. Mahogany and fabric. England. 19th c.

Night tables. Mahogany and various woods. England. 19th c.

Paintings and Prints

Portrait of a gentleman. Painting. Artist unknown. Oil on canvas. 19th c.

George Washington Vanderbilt, Frederick William Vanderbilt, and Eliza Osgood Vanderbilt. Depicted as children. Painting. Jacob H. Lazarus (1822–1891). Oil on canvas. United States. 1867.

Portrait of two young boys. Painting. Artist unknown. Oil on canvas. 1850.

Seascape. Painting. M. Becketin. Oil on canvas. 19th c.

Harold Stirling Vanderbilt. Miniature portrait. Antoine Oderica after Ch. Chaplin. 19th c.

Maude S. and Aldine. Print. Currier & Ives. United States. ca. 1885.

Decorative Objects

Desk set. Meissen. Porcelain. 19th c.

Compote. Cie. Boucheron. Enameled metal. Palais Royal, France. 19th c.

Clock. Mahogany, glass, and brass. Case made in England. ca. 1800. Works made in France. ca. 1850.

Pair of candlesticks. Rock crystal and ormolu. France. 19th c.

Inkwell. Brass and marble. France. 19th c.

Letter openers. Ivory. ca. 1900.

Lamp. Ceramic. Late 19th early 20th c.

Mrs. George Washington Vanderbilt. Photographs. Copies of 19th c. originals.

Photograph frame. Brass and glass. ca. 1895.

Rug. Wool and cotton. Khurassan region, Persia. 19th c.

Rug. Wool and cotton. Hamadan region, Persia. Late 19th c.

SHERATON–CHIPPENDALE BATHROOM

Dressing table. Painted wood and marble. England. 19th c.

Chairs. Painted wood. United States. 19th c.

Laundry hamper. Wicker. 19th c.

Table and step stool. Painted wood. 19th c.

Pitchers. Brass. 19th c.

CHIPPENDALE ROOM

Furniture

Tester bed. Mahogany. England. 19th c. Chippendale style.

Wardrobe. Cuban mahogany. England. ca. 1760. Neoclassical.

Settee, armchairs, and side chairs. Mahogany and fabric. England. 18th and 19th c. Chippendale style.

Pair of candlestands. Mahogany. England. Early 19th c.

Night table. Mahogany. England. ca. 1760–1770.

Desk and drop-leaf table. Mahogany. England. 19th c.

Magazine stand. Painted leather. 19th c.

Side table. England. 19th c.

Paintings

Young Algerian Girl. Painting. Pierre-Auguste Renoir (1841–1919). Oil on canvas. France. ca. 1881.

Child with an Orange. Painting. Pierre-Auguste Renoir (1841–1919). Oil on canvas. France. ca. 1881.

Watercolor by Lady William Cecil, early 20th century.
HALLWAY OUTSIDE SHERATON ROOM.

Sortie du Port-Temps Lumineux.
   Painting. Maxime Maufra (1861–
   1918). Oil on canvas. ca. 1894.
View of Harbor in Sunset. Painting.
   Maxime Maufra (1861–1918).
   Oil on canvas. ca. 1900.
Watercolors. Lady William Cecil
   (1857–1919). England.
   Early 20th c.

Decorative Objects

Fire screen. Enameled leaded glass
   and rosewood. United States.
   ca. 1895.
Clock. Matthew Hill. Mahogany
   and brass. England. ca. 1790.
Pair of candlesticks. Brass.
   France. 18th c.
Vases. Stoneware with Celadon
   glaze. Ch'ien-lung reign, China.
   Ch'ing Dynasty (1736–1796).
Covered containers. Enamel and
   metal. Probably China. 19th c.
Stamps. Soapstone. Probably
   China. 19th c.
Figure of cat. Ceramic and wood.
   Probably China. 19th c.
Bed warmer. Brass and copper.
   Probably United States. 19th c.
Andirons and fireplace set. Brass.
   19th c.
Lamps. Ceramic, glass, and metal.
   19th c.
Magazines. Paper. Early 20th c.
Fan. Fabric, wood, feathers,
   and paint. Asia. 19th c.
Stationary portfolio. Leather. 19th c.

Wooden ball and tenpins,
Brunswick-Balke-Collender
Company, 19th century.
BOWLING ALLEY.

CHIPPENDALE–OLD
ENGLISH BATHROOM

Washstand. Wood and marble.
   England. 19th c.
Chairs and mirror. Painted wood.
   United States. 19th c.
Towel rack. Mahogany. 19th c.
Laundry hamper. Wicker. 19th c.

OLD ENGLISH ROOM
Furniture
Bed. Brass. England. 19th c.
Settee, armchairs, and side chairs.
   Fabric and oak. England.
   19th c. Knole style.
Gateleg table. Oak. England. 17th c.
Chests of drawers. Oak. England.
   19th c. Jacobean style.
Cupboard. Oak. 19th c.
   Renaissance revival style.
Chest-on-stand. Wood. England.
   17th c.

Stools. Wood. Biltmore Estate
   Industries. Asheville, North
   Carolina. ca. 1906–1917.
   Gothic style.
Cupboard. Wood. 19th c. Gothic
   style.

Paintings and Prints
Sir William Cecil, 1st Lord Burghley.
   Painting. Marcus Gheeraerts
   the Younger (1561–1636).
   Oil on canvas. Flanders. 1589.
*Honorable John Francis Amherst
   Cecil.* Painting. W. I. Cox
   (1900–54). Oil on canvas.
   ca. 1920.
*William Cecil, 2nd Earl of
   Salisbury, and Frances Cecil.*
   Depicted as children. Painting.
   Frederico Zuccaro (1543–1609).
   Oil on canvas. Italy. 1599.
Prints of English nobility. William
   Fiathorne. 17th c.

Decorative Objects
Candelabra. Brass. 19th c.
Walking or hunting seat. Wood,
   leather, and metal. United States.
   19th c.
Inlaid box. Brass and enamel.
   Possibly Persia. 19th c.
The Browsing Stag. Sculpture.
   Pierre-Jules Mêne (1810–1871).
   Bronze. France. 19th c.
Steins. Burlwood. Netherlands. 18th c.
Vase. Stoneware with celadon glaze.
   Ch'ien-lung reign, China.
   Ch'ing Dynasty (1736–1796).
Teapot. Pewter and wood. France.
   18th to 19th c.
Clock. Andrew Flockart. Ebonized
   wood, brass, and other metals.
   London, England. ca. 1820.
Figures of parrots. Porcelain and gilt
   bronze. 19th c.
Fireplace accessories. Metal. 19th c.
Fireplace screen. Embroidered canvas
   and wood. United States. 19th c.

BASEMENT STAIRWELL
AND LANDING
Frieze section. Plaster. 19th c.
Trestle table. Wood and iron. Spain.

BOWLING ALLEY
Sofa and club chairs. Fabric and
   wood. England. 19th c.
Tables. Wood. Late 19th–early
   20th c. Baroque style.
Table tennis table. Oak. United
   States. Late 19th c.

Table tennis set. Wood, leather, and
   net. United States. Late 19th c.
Dish. Ceramic. United States. 20th c.
Dulcitone player piano. Cable
   Nelson Piano Co. Chicago,
   Illinois. Late 19th–early 20th c.
Piano bench. Wood. United States.
   Late 19th–early 20th century.
Bowling balls and pins.
   United States. ca. 1895.
Score-keeping board. Painted
   Wood. Brunswick-Balke-
   Collender Company.
   United States. ca. 1895.
Friezes. Plaster. 19th c. casts.
George Washington Vanderbilt.
   Bust. Marble. Mary Grant.
   Scotland. ca. 1889.
Photogravures of (left to right) *Night
   and Dawn* by Michelangelo,
   Venus de Milo, the *Sistine Chapel
   Ceiling* by Michelangelo, *Nike of
   Samothrace, St. George* by
   Donatello, *David* and *Lorenzo de
   Medici* by Michelangelo.
   Late 19th–early 20th c.

SITTING AREA
Savonarola chairs. Oak. Italy. 19th c.
Gateleg table. Walnut. Late 19th–
   early 20th c.
Trestle table. Oak. 19th c.
Settee. Oak. 19th c.
Lamps. Ceramic and brass.
   England. 19th c.
Photogravures. Late 19th–early 20th c.

DRESSING ROOMS
Towel racks. Mahogany. 19th c.
Cabinets. Oak. 19th c.
Side chairs. Designer, Richard
   Morris Hunt (1828–1895).
   Maker, Baumgarten & Co.
   Wood. New York. ca. 1895.
Bowls and pitchers. Minton.
   Porcelain. England. ca. 1895.
Hairbrushes. Wood and bristles.
   20th c.
Towels. Cotton. 19th and 20th c.

MAIN DRESSING ROOM
AND MAIN BATH
Towel racks. Mahogany, painted
   wood and caning. 19th c.
Dressing table. Mahogany.
   England. 19th c.
Side chair. Various woods and rush.
   19th c. Sheraton style.
Cheval mirror. Wood and glass. 19th c.
Traveling toilet set. Various
   materials 19th c.
Water bottles. Glass. 19th c.

Bottle. Glass. 19th c.
Toilet sets. Minton. Porcelain.
England. ca. 1895.
Towels. Cotton. 19th and 20th c.

DRESSING ROOM LOUNGE

Settee and side chairs. Walnut and
caning. England. 19th c.
Baroque style.
Gateleg table. Wood.
Late 19th–early 20th c.
Photogravures. Late 19th–early
20th c.

GYMNASIUM

Parallel bars, exercise machines,
and Indian clubs. Wood and
metal. A. G. Spalding & Bro.
United States. 19th c.
Dumbbells. Wood. 19th c.
Gym scale. Fairbanks. Metal. 19th c.
Cabinet. Oak and glass. 19th c.
Fencing equipment. Leather and
metal. Late 19th–early 20th c.
Medicine ball. Leather.
Late 19th–early 20th c.
Rowing machine. Wood and metal.
Late 19th–early 20th c.
Towels. Cotton. 20th c.
Towel rack. Mahogany. 19th c.

HOUSEKEEPER'S PANTRY

Work table and stools. Wood. 19th c.
Barrel. Wood and metal.
Late 19th–early 20th c.
Oil lamp. Glass and metal. 19th c.
Inkwell. Glass. Early 20th c.
Rug beater. Metal and wood.
Early 20th c.
Food cans. Paper and metal. 20th c.
reproductions. Labels reproduced
from the collection of Ralph and
Terry Kovel, Cleveland, Ohio.
Special thanks to United States
Can Co. for its contribution of
custom cans.

WALK-IN REFRIGERATORS

Fruit crate labels. 20th c.
reproductions.
Milk cans. 20th c.
Special thanks to White Rock
Bottling Co. for providing period
Sparkling Water bottles for display.

CANNING PANTRY

Step stool. Wood. 19th c.
"XXth Century" cooler. Cordley and
Hayes. Ceramic and metal.
New York. 20th c.
Oil lamps. Glass and metal. 19th
and 20th c.
Box. Metal. 19th c.
Various canning equipment.
Late 19th–20th c.

SERVANTS' BEDROOMS

Chests of drawers, mirrors, and
bedside tables. Chestnut. United
States. 19th c.
Wardrobe. Oak and glass. 19th c.
Beds and washstands. Painted iron
and brass. United States. 19th c.
Rockers and side chairs. Wood.
United States. 19th c.
Toilet accessories. Minton.
Porcelain. England. ca. 1895.
Servants' clothing. 19th c.
Towels. Cotton. 20th c.
Prints. 19th and 20th centuries.

PASTRY KITCHEN

Table and chairs. Wood. 19th c.
Ovens. Branhall, Deane & Co.,
New York. Metal. Late 19th c.
Refrigerator. Lorillard. New York.
Wood and metal. Late 19th c.
Universal bread maker. Landers, Fray
& Clark. Metal. New Britain,
Connecticut. 1904.
Scale. Brass and iron. United States
Cutlery Co. Late 19th c.
Dessert plates. Garnet glass and
gilding. 19th c.
Various cooking equipment.
19th and 20th c.
Food cans. Paper and metal.
20th c. reproductions. Labels
reproduced from the collection of
Ralph and Terry Kovel,
Cleveland, Ohio. Special thanks
to United States Can Co. for its
contribution of custom cans.

ROTISSERIE KITCHEN

Work table. Oak. Late 19th c.
Cabinet. Metal. Late 19th c.
Rotisserie. Branhall, Deane & Co.
New York. ca. 1895.
Pot. Copper. 20th c.
Mortar and pestle. Marble. 19th c.
Fireplace accessories. Iron. 20th c.
Towel. Linen. 19th c.

MAIN KITCHEN

Tables and chairs. Wood. Late 19th c.
Ovens, pots, and pans. Branhall,
Deane & Co. New York. Metal.
ca. 1895.
Storage cabinet. Steel. Duparquet,
Huot, & Moneuse. New York.
Metal. ca. 1895.
Butcher block. Wood and metal.
20th c.
Serving cart. A. Bertuch. Metal.
Berlin, Germany. 19th c.
Coffee mill. Enterprise
Manufacturing Co. Philadelphia,
Pennsylvania. Metal and wood.
Patent Oct. 21, 1873.
Sausage stuffer. Enterprise
Manufacturing Co. Philadelphia,
Pennsylvania. Metal and wood.
Late 19th c.
Food chopping machine. Metal.
United States. Late 19th c.
Mortar and pestal. Marble and wood.
19th c.
Food cans. Paper and metal.
20th c. reproductions. Labels
reproduced from the collection of
Ralph and Terry Kovel,
Cleveland, Ohio. Special thanks
to United States Can Co. for its
contribution of custom cans.

KITCHEN PANTRY

In Dumbwaiters:

Trays. Wood and metal. 19th c.
Breakfast ware. Minton. Porcelain.
England. ca. 1896.
Breakfast ware. Spode-Copeland.
Porcelain. England. ca. 1896.
Tumbler. Baccarat. Crystal. France.
Early 20th c. "CSV" monogram.
Napkin. Linen. 19th c.
Flatware. Silverplate. 20th c.

In Cabinets:

Plates, cups, and saucers. Mercer.
Ceramic. England. ca. 1924.
Sugar dishes. Wedgwood. Ceramic.
20th c.
Water pitchers. Glass. 20th c.

SERVANTS' DINING ROOM

Sideboard. J. & J. W. Meeks.
Rosewood and marble. New York.
19th c.
Side chairs. Wood and caning. 19th c.
Sideboard. Oak. 19th c. Mission style.
Dining table. Mahogany. 19th c.
Gong and beater. Brass, wood, and
fabric. England. 1896.

Oil lamps. Glass and metal.
19th and 20th c.
Water pitchers. Late 19th–early 20th c.
Prints. 20th c.

SERVANTS' SITTING ROOM

Drop-front desk. Biltmore Estate
Industries. Oak. Asheville,
North Carolina. ca. 1906–1917.
Rockers with splint seats and backs.
L. J. Colony, Keene, New
Hampshire. Late 19th–
early 20th c.
Sideboard, chairs, tables, bric-a-brac
shelf, book shelf, hat rack. United
States. 19th c.
Victrola phonograph. Victor Talking
Machine Co. Wood and metal.
Camden, New Jersey. Early 20th c.
Model VV–IX. Hand-cranked.
Autoharp. Zimmerman Autoharp
Co. Ebonized wood and metal.
Dolgeville, New York.
Oil lamp. Glass and metal. 19th c.
Checkerboard. Painted wood.
ca. 1900.
Decorative objects and books.
Various materials. 19th and 20th c.
Prints. 20th c.

SMALL PANTRY

Cans, boxes, and barrels. Late 19th c.,
and late 20th c. reproductions.
Special thanks to Nabisco,
Morton Salt, Del Monte,
Wm. Underwood Co., and Jerry
and Audry Glenn for providing
items for display.

BROWN LAUNDRY

Table and chairs. Wood. 19th c.
Washer. The Boss Washing Machine
Co. Wood and metal. Cincinnati,
Ohio. Early 20th c.
Wringer. "Kingston" Anchor brand,
Lovell Manufacturing Co. Wood,
metal, and rubber. United States.
Late 19th–early 20th c.
"Old Time" wringer. The United
States Wringer Co. Wood, metal,
and rubber. Patent March 27,
1888.
Table-size dampening press. United
States. Wood and fabric. 20th c.
Washboards, irons, fluters, and
laundry aids. 19th and 20th c.
Pot-bellied stove. Iron. United
States. Late 19th–early 20th c.
Hamper. Wood. Late 19th–early
20th c.

LAUNDRESSES' TOILET

Washstand. Painted iron. Late 19th c.
Rockers. Wood. 19th c.
Bowl and pitcher. Minton. Porcelain. England. Late 19th c.

MAIN LAUNDRY

Table and chairs. Wood. 19th c.
Mangle. Metal and wood. Algonquin, Illinois. 20th c.
Extractor. Metal and leather. The United States Laundry Machinery Co. 20th c.
Barrel washer. Metal. Troy Laundry Machinery Co. ca. 1907.
Washboard, wringers, and laundry aids. United States. 19th and 20th c.

DRYING ROOM

Drying racks. Wood and metal. Troy Laundry Machinery Co. 1895.
Bed sheets. Cotton. United States. 20th c.
Work table. Wood. United States. Late 19th c.
Laundry aids. United States. 19th and 20th c.

STAIRWELL TO BACHELORS'S WING

Frieze sections. Plaster. 19th c.
Photogravures. Late 19th–early 20th c.
Taxidermic specimens. 19th c.

SMOKING ROOM

Furniture

Table. Petrified wood and bronze. France. 19th c.
Sofas and chairs. Fabric and wood. England. 19th c. Knole style.
Pembroke table. Mahogany. 19th c.
Pembroke table with painted decoration. Edwards & Roberts. Mahogany and paint. London, England. 19th c.
Bureau. Walnut. 19th c.
Side chair. Walnut. Spain. 19th c.

Decorative Objects

Pipe rack. Burled walnut and brass. 19th c.
Kovsh (drinking vessel). Metal. Russia. 19th c.

Pipe rack, English, 19th century.
SMOKING ROOM.

Pipes. Wood and metal. 19th and 20th c.
Tobacco tins. Copper and pewter. 19th c.
Clock. Mahogany and metal. France. ca. 1850–1880.
Jugs. Majolica ceramic. 19th c.
Desk set. Delft ceramic. Netherlands. 19th c.
Elephant group. Lacquerware and ivory. 19th c.
Lamp. Earthenware and metal. Japan. 19th c.
Taxidermic specimens. 19th c.
Rug. Wool. Bidjar region, Persia. 19th c.
Queen Charlotte, Duke of York, Hamilton, Lavater, Shakespeare, Empress of Russia, Lord Nelson, Herschel, Pope, Captain Cook. Framed portrait medallions. Wedgwood. Jasperware. England. 18th c.
Framed medallion with classical scene. Wedgwood. Jasperware. England. 18th c.

GUN ROOM

Furniture

Pedestal table. Marble and wood. United States. 19th c.
Armchairs. Fabric and wood. 19th c.
Side chairs. Walnut. Spain. 19th c.
Table with drawer and twist-turned legs. Walnut and various woods. 17th c.
Side table. Wood. England. 18th c.

Prints

Engravings. Sir Joshua Reynolds (1723–1792), after George Morland (1763–1804), William Ward (1766–1826), Samuel William Reynolds (1773–1835), and James Ward (1769–1859). England. 18th c.

Decorative Objects

Game boxes and chips. Tiffany & Co. Wood, metal, and mother-of-pearl. United States. 19th c.
Roulette wheel. Wood and metal. 19th c.
Clock. Various woods and brass. England. ca. 1810.

Fox Chasing a Rabbit. Sculpture. Joseph-Victor Chemin (1825–1901). Bronze. France. 19th c.
Lioness. Sculpture. Antoine-Louis Barye (1796–1875). Bronze. France. 19th c.
Panting Female Dog "Milla" and *Buck and Doe.* Sculpture. Pierre-Jules Mêne (1810–1871). Bronze. France. 19th c.
Trophy. Sterling silver. United States. 1903.
Pipe holder with goat heads. Wood. 19th c.
Lamps. Marble. Early 20th c.
Fireplace accessories. Metal. 19th c.
Taxidermic specimens. Late 19th and 20th c.
Rug. Wool. Karabagh region, Caucasus. 19th c.
Rug. Wool. Qashgai region, Persia. 19th c.

BACHELORS' HALLWAY

Furniture

Armchairs. Leather and wood. England. 19th c. Jacobean style.
Gateleg table. Wood. United States. 19th c.
Cabinet. Oak. 19th c. Provincial Louis XV style.
Renaissance credenza and matching stands. Walnut and marble. 19th c.
Small chest. Mahogany and brass. 19th c.
Armchair. Leather, wood, and metal. Spain or Portugal.

Paintings and Prints

Architectural prints. Axel Herman Haig (1838–1921). Sweden. 19th c.

Decorative Objects

Victrola Phonograph. Victor Talking Machine Co. Wood and metal. Camden, New Jersey. Early 20th c.
Phonograph record. Columbia Masterworks. Plastic. United States. 20th c.
Taxidermic specimens. United States. Late 19th and late 20th c.